LIFE IN THE SLOW LANE

LIFE IN THE SLOW LANE

Margaret Tessler

To order additional copies of this book, contact:
Xlibris Corporation
1-888-795-4274
www.Xlibris.com
Orders@Xlibris.com
22878

To our children (Howard's four and my five), their spouses, and all the grandchildren in our blended family. We love you all and thank you for sharing our dream!

ACKNOWLEDGMENTS

I owe a big debt of gratitude to all the RVers, campground hosts, and helpful townspeople who contributed to the joy of our adventures. Compiling these tales has brought to mind many friendly faces and happy memories.

In addition, I greatly appreciate all the editorial help I got from Chris Ketcham, Louise Gibson, Jerry Aguirre, Ed Jones, and members of my writing groups: George Anderson, Dave Bachelor, Mel Eisenstadt, Edie Flaherty, Jeanne Knight, Betsy Lackmann, Jan McConaghy, Helen Pilz, Ronda Sofia, and Mary Zerbe. I could never have written this without their invaluable feedback.

Thanks, too, to my publicist, Karen Villanueva, who encourages me every step of the way.

Most of all, thanks to my husband, who not only enjoyed reliving the travels with me, but filled in the gaps where my memory faltered.

INTRODUCTION

"You won't last six weeks," grumbled one pessimist.

"How can you live without a *house*?" worried my husband's father, who had lived in apartments all his life.

My parents wore brave, bewildered smiles.

"Go for it!" encouraged our kids.

And go for it we did. When Howard and I retired in 1990, we put our house on the market, then sold, gave away, or stored most of our belongings. In January of 1991, we moved into our thirty-foot Alpenlite fifth-wheel trailer, hitched it to our Ford truck, and set out to tour the country.

This wasn't a spur-of-the-moment decision. We'd planned, studied, budgeted, and investigated RVs in and out of Albuquerque for over three years before making the leap that—up till then—others had considered only a vague daydream.

Our full-time adventure lasted nearly eight years. While on the road, I wrote letters to family and friends telling about the funny—and not so funny—things we experienced, people we met, and discoveries we made.

In consolidating these tales, I've omitted huge quantities of material that would have been of interest only to our family. However I've also *kept* some family stories, simply because they seemed relevant, or humorous, or because, after all, our families are such an integral part of our lives.

I've also eliminated the adjective "beautiful" a few thousand times (but not altogether). So—unless I say otherwise—just assume our stops were scenic.

May you enjoy the reading as much as we enjoyed the traveling.

1989

WILLOW CREEK CAMPGROUND
HERON LAKE, NEW MEXICO
July 7-10, 1989

Before making the leap to "full-timing," we decided to test the idea with short vacation trips. The first Saturday after buying our new Alpenlite, we spent the morning (or forty-five minutes of it) in the parking lot of Smith's grocery store, with Howard practicing his backing-up skills while I practiced knee-bends, arm-waving, and shouting. We quickly realized that using walkie-talkies would do great things for our patience—to say nothing of my knees, arms, and voice.

The next day we took a rousing sixty-mile round-trip all the way from Albuquerque to the neighboring town of Moriarity and back. Then Captain Grandpa decided we were ready for the big time and picked the weekend of his birthday for our first journey. I updated my will, and we set out for Heron Lake near Chama, New Mexico.

So here I am—Lieutenant Grandma—reporting on our maiden voyage. Now that we're here, I hope to learn some helpful RV techniques by watching the people across from us as they set up camp. What I've learned so far is that their names are Oma and Opa (who are probably in their late sixties) and Timmy (who's about seven or eight).

Timmy and Oma have been shouting directions to Opa as he backs their fifth-wheel in. Now that the RV is parked, Opa has begun parking the boat next to it. At this very moment, the nose of his truck is pointed downhill, straight at our dinette (where I'm sitting). We hope he does well, don't we. Maybe I should go out and help Timmy and Oma shout. I'm well-practiced.

They also have a teeny tiny white poodle named Taffy. I heard Timmy ask Taffy if he'd run into a skunk. So. He noticed.

But now that Opa has the trailer leveled and the awning out, it will take more than a mere skunk to drive them away.

We seasoned RVers learn to adapt.

1990 & 1991

ALBUQUERQUE, NEW MEXICO
JOURNAL ENTRIES—December 1990

December 21: Snow!
December 22: More snow!
December 25: Frozen holding tanks.
December 28: Even more snow!

DEL RIO, TEXAS—January 17-23, 1991

We'd taken a few *vacation* trips in our Alpenlite since that initial trip to Heron Lake, but this was the first trip we took as "full-timers." After an unusually cold and snowy December in Albuquerque, we eagerly headed south to Del Rio for a few balmy weeks.

Traffic was sparse from Carlsbad, New Mexico, where we spent the first night. Scenery was almost as sparse. Brownish-gray mountains jutted along the horizon like cardboard backdrops to the dull-green patches of vegetation dotting the sandy landscape.

Just as we came to a "deer crossing" sign south of Fort Stockton, Texas, a deer leapt across the road directly in front of us—almost as if he'd been hiding behind this sign, waiting to play a game of "chicken" with passing motorists. Fortunately he made it across, so I guess we both won.

Turning east at Sanderson, we were treated to another change in scenery. From there to Del Rio we took in miles of velvety silvery-leafed purple sage, mingling in striking contrast to the thorny blackbrush growing alongside it.

When we arrived in Del Rio, the weather was delightful. But sometime during the night it started raining, and the rain continued for three days. When the sun finally broke through, it changed the color of everything, including our mood. Del Rio is on the Amistad Reservoir, a large lake that was pewter gray under the clouds, and royal blue under the sun.

Sunday, after our one day of sunshine and warmth, the weather turned cold and cloudy again. Years ago, when we went to Phoenix every June, I used to remind the kids that summer—everywhere—is hot. Now Howard and I are having to remind ourselves that January—everywhere—is cold.

We decided to brave the gray skies and cool breezes and venture into town to take the "walking tour." Besides admiring the charming homes and picturesque courthouse square, I was also elated to find an old-fashioned Kress. I don't know why these old "five-and-dimes" fascinate me so. Maybe it's the hard-to-find contrast to the shiny modern superstores. Maybe it's because they aren't quaint or rustic by design; they're just naturally that way. Maybe it's because I feel as if I've stepped backward in time; I half-expect to find Ipana toothpaste on the shelves, or the small aqua-colored tubes of lipstick I used to buy when I was in junior high school.

We often think of family and friends and wonder what Albuquerque is like since January 16th and the beginning of Desert Storm. In Del Rio, we saw yellow ribbons of all sizes on homes, stores, and cars. Not only did billboards ask for prayers for *all* our troops, but for individual servicemen by name, and we felt sure everyone in town knew who they were.

ZAPATA, TEXAS
January 23 through February 10, 1991

We finally decided the weather we weren't going to talk about had stayed cold long enough and perhaps we should head further south. On our way to the Equator, we found ourselves here in Zapata.

When we arrived at Bass Lake RV Park, the weather was ideal, but I had some misgivings about the "wildlife." While Howard went to the office to register, I waited in the car, watching a myriad of mosquito-like insects plaster themselves to the windshield. I wondered if we'd last the night.

But the winged critters turned out to be non-mosquitoes with absolutely no interest in us. The one night turned into a week, the week into three weeks. We'd have stayed indefinitely if we hadn't needed to return to Albuquerque for family matters.

Our designated site was between a couple of fat palm trees, and Howard had to negotiate between them to get us situated. The park manager hadn't had much practice directing fifth-wheels in the tricky art of backing up, but gave it her cheerful best. Meanwhile, our next-door neighbor came out to offer his arm-waving and general helpfulness.

At one point, as Howard was half-in, half-out, at a strange angle and blocking the road, Neighbor said, "Wait, I know just what you need." This was good news. Maybe he'd help us get parked before nightfall. Then Neighbor hurried closer, peered in the window and proceeded to tell Howard, not about parking, but about a brand of tailgate we could have installed that would help cut down on gas mileage. While Neighbor went inside his rig to get some brochures on the subject, Howard somehow managed to get us parked where we needed to be.

Our site was only a few hundred yards from the lake, and once settled, we had a lovely tropical view.

January 31, 1991

We've been getting to know our neighbors and enjoying park activities. Exercise classes take place in the clubhouse three mornings a week, but I've hesitated about going, since I have neither a designer sweatband nor a designer body. But I heard we exercise to the tunes of Julio Iglesias, so I thought "what the heck," hauled out my basic black sweat pants with matching T-shirt, and trotted over.

There weren't many of us, nobody looked real chic, and our instructor was overcoming a severe physical handicap and rebuilding her own stamina little by little while leading the group. What an inspiration!

Tuesday it turned HOT. I read in yesterday's paper that (1) the nation's high, in Hollywood, Florida, was 85°, and (2) the high in Laredo, forty-eight miles north of us, was 88°. Hmm. I'm amazed at my own ignorance regarding Laredo. All these years I've pictured it as a small dusty town populated solely by cowboys (some of them wrapped up in white linen). What a surprise to discover it's a relatively large (population 108,000+), modern, bustling city. We considered staying there, but decided we wanted something a little more low-key.

Zapata (population about 3500) is definitely low-key. Yesterday was an eventful day: The garbage was collected. To understand the significance of this, you need to know it was a week overdue because *both* garbage trucks had broken down. Everyone in town breathed a sigh of relief when they were repaired.

We were excited because we found a deli in town. Deli = bagels, right? No bagels, but marvelous cinnamon rolls. If not bagels, there are other familiar things: Registration for Little League. High-school basketball games. Pizza Hut.

Wednesday it turned *very* cold—just to keep us from gloating too much, I guess. Today—maybe I should see what the paper says before taking a definite stand on this, but I'll risk it—today is a glorious day.

February 6, 1991

There are certain nitty-gritty realities that impinge on our nomadic lifestyle. Howard's father wasn't the only one concerned by our lack of roots. Not knowing our whereabouts made the IRS and bill collectors nervous as well.

We knew we eventually wanted to make Texas our legal residence. Before leaving Albuquerque, we chose a mail-forwarding service based in Texas. After arriving in Zapata, we decided to take another preliminary step by acquiring a Texas ID through the Motor Vehicle Department. None of our neighbors knew where it was, so we went to the County Courthouse for information.

"Well," mused the young woman at the desk with a puzzled expression, "I think they do that at the Lions Club on Wednesdays."

So today, since it's Wednesday, we went to the Lions Club, where the MVD had set up an office. A state trooper was the only person running it. We were quite impressed with his efficiency. He didn't waste time, but also gave the impression of being unhurried. Courteous and patient, he was "the everything"—the written-test-giver, the driving-test-giver, the eye-test-giver, the typist, the photographer, the receptionist.

We had to wait about forty-five minutes for our turn, but at least we got to wait sitting down. And it wasn't any longer than our last wait in Albuquerque, standing in six separate lines, waited on by six grumpy people.

Despite the shortage of bagels, coming here was a good move. I *love* this place. We're as happy as clams! (I'm not sure how clams got this reputation for being so jovial, but we'll assume it's so.) Howard inflated our boat and leaves it down by the lake, which is almost outside our door. He goes fishing whenever he feels like it without much fuss or bother. I can sit here at my computer and look out the window at the lake and birds. We take walks together, or chat with the neighbors, or sit outside on our lawn chairs and read.

One couple we like a lot are Audrey and Dude Cain from Idaho. Dude's an ex-police chief and a fly fisherman. He's a big burly guy, and everyone's surprised to discover he's also an artist who has done some beautifully intricate watercolors.

We've also had fun exchanging stories with the people next door. They told us about another group of people they've come to admire: Little old ladies in their mid-eighties who drive enormous RVs across the country all alone.

ALBUQUERQUE, NEW MEXICO
Mid-February through July 4, 1991

We returned to Albuquerque to be near Howard's father, who was terminally ill. We had good times being with family and friends, and sad times as we watched Papa slowly fade away. The wonderful Hospice volunteers made this time easier for all of us. Papa died June 3, and we remained here with family for a while, giving each other emotional support.

CHAMA, NEW MEXICO—July 5-11, 1991

By the first of July, we felt ready to begin our journey again. This is another perfect town for us "Tessler Turtles." I think it might be even more laid back than Zapata. (Zapata had a Dairy Queen *and* a Pizza Hut; Chama boasts only a Dairy Queen.) We found a ("a" as in "only one") tennis court by the school. If two other people in town want to use it, we're out of luck. But it's in good condition and usually not busy, so we've played at tennis a couple of afternoons.

The oldest hotel in town has been here since 1881 and looks every day of it. The dining room has a cozy pot-bellied stove where the *viejos* (old-timers) gather to exchange stories. We used to love going there for breakfast whenever we came to Chama to cross-country ski. And we still enjoy Vera's Restaurant, where we celebrated Howard's birthday on the 8th.

We're staying in a nice campground (Rio Chama Campground) in the middle of a wooded area. We're also right by the Chama River and the Cumbres-Toltec railroad line. Some people go down to the river to fish, some to swim, and some just to look around. The narrow-gauge train comes by twice a day: in the morning on the way to Antonito, and in the late afternoon on the way back.

Whenever it's due, people from the campground gather by the tracks to take pictures and/or wave at the people on the train, who wave back with equal enthusiasm. I don't know why this is so much fun, but it somehow establishes a camaraderie, making the world a friendlier place.

So many chipmunks occupy the park, we nearly step on them when we step outside. That is, until Howard sets up his camera to catch them in action. Then they suddenly remember they have another engagement and disappear. Otherwise, they're fun to watch, the babies scuffling with each other the way kittens and puppies play.

The hummingbirds flock to our feeder, and we've also seen numerous magpies while walking into town. And the flowers—wildflowers, columbines, and poppies—are everywhere. The sweet yellow clover, especially, gives off a heavenly fragrance. We're less than eight miles from the Colorado border, so maybe that's why we see so many "Colorado" flowers/birds.

In the midst of all this primitive stuff, we've been enjoying some of the benefits of modern technology ("modern" being a relative term). We've used our electric blanket on chilly mountain nights. And we watched Steffi Graf and Michael Stich win at Wimbledon on TV.

We get only one TV channel, so we watch the *Today* show and the local news in order to keep up with whatever mayhem is going on in the world and in Albuquerque. Since we can't get our favorite other-channel shows, we watch videos we'd taped earlier. Right now, it's Ken Burns's fascinating *Civil War* series.

Can't help wondering how not only American history, but our own family history, would have been altered if events had taken a different turn at any number of points along the way. (Would my Yankee grandmother have even met my Southern grandfather if they'd lived in two separate countries?)

Back to the present. Don't you hear that whistle blowing? Gotta go meet the train!

CREEDE, COLORADO—July 12-21, 1991

Several years ago we passed through Creede, a quaint old mining town, and liked it so much we'd always wanted to come back. On the way here this time, we consulted our campground directories and found an RV park that looked inviting. The average space width was listed as sixty feet (which is more than twice what most places have). The park was described as "grassy."

When we first saw it Friday afternoon, our hearts sank. It was just a huge field with RVs lined up all in a row (rather four rows).

"Grassy," we're learning, means "no trees"—and the grass ain't necessarily green.

And those sixty-foot spaces the directory described so enticingly were laid out funny. Two RVs shared one electric pole, so on one side, you could practically spit in your neighbor's window (if you were so inclined). On the opposite side, however, a hundred feet stretched between you and your other neighbor.

Once we got settled in, we realized our first impression was misleading. We were parked near the end, and our Siamese-twin neighbors were pleasant and unobtrusive (they didn't spit). The other side was, of course, *very* roomy, and from the back window (the living room area), we could see hummingbirds at our feeder, as well as *green, green* mountains and trees in the background.

We discovered there are twice as many tennis courts in Creede as in Chama—meaning, there are two courts. However one court has tall weeds growing on it. The other slants, but once we got used to standing slantwise, we enjoyed playing.

We stopped to chat with the only other RVers with New Mexico license plates. Nearly everyone else was from Texas or Oklahoma. Sunday morning while Howard went fishing, I went to church with our newfound New Mexico friends. When I came home, I saw that new neighbors had pulled in on the "faraway" side of our RV site.

Seeing their Arizona license plates, I went bounding right over to be neighborly. There I found two men who had just finished sorting out their fishing gear and were in the midst of pitching a tent under the awning of their trailer. It quickly dawned on me they were batching it and not overly delighted to see me.

Not that they weren't polite; they even called off their dog. But it must have been that look of panic in their eyes that alerted me. I think they weren't sure if I was someone's wayward wife, or merely some fanatic about to inflict my particular brand of religion on them. In either case, they looked ready to take flight.

So I retreated, minded my own business for the rest of the day, and watched the hummingbirds. We had three different "regulars": one rubythroated, one bright green, and one bright-orange rufous.

Later, when we had to take down the feeder, the hummers were perturbed and kept flying to the spot where the feeder used to be. I was glad they could turn to other neighbors after we left.

GUNNISON AREA, COLORADO
July 22-31, 1991

We're enjoying cool weather—and quite a bit of rain. Lovely weather for watching videos. When it's not raining, we're usually hiking.

I decided that since I enjoy wildflower-watching so much, I should learn the names of the flowers. What a can of worms that turned out to be! The ones I see never look like anything in my guidebook and vice versa. Besides that, a lot of pretty little wildflowers have such ugly names, I wonder if the botanists were in a grumpy mood when they made them up.

But my guidebook says that using the scientific name will eliminate vagueness and confusion. Well, let's give it a try:

Margaret: Oh, Howard, look at this beautiful Scrophulariacea.
Howard: Wash your mouth out with soap, woman.
Margaret: But, honey, I'm eliminating vagueness and confusion!

So much for that. Let's try the English version:

Margaret: Oh, Howard, look at this darlin' beardtongue penstemon of the figwort family.
Howard: Glad you cleared that up.

Did you know that the Latin name for the Utah penstemon is "penstemon utahensis"? Now isn't that something! Those ancient Romans were clever enough to figure out a Latin name for an American Indian word that would someday be applied to a simple little wildflower! Did you know that the "Linum Lewisii" was named for Meriwether Lewis of the Lewis and Clark expedition? Another example of the farsightedness of those cagey old Romans.

*   *   *

After we left Monarch Valley Ranch (26 miles *east* of Gunnison), we traveled all the way to Blue Mesa Ranch (12 miles *west* of Gunnison). We seldom travel more than 220 miles a day, if that many, so this was a new low.

We'd found a flyer on our windshield inviting us to spend two nights at Blue Mesa "free"—in exchange for listening to a pitch to join their home park as well as Camp-Coast-to-Coast (CCC), a nationwide camping network. We figured we'd spend our two free nights and run, but surprised ourselves by signing up.

In return, Howard got a cap with the Blue Mesa logo—a hat he calls his $4,000 hat. Well, yes, there were other perks. We can stay free at Blue Mesa or its sister park, Twin Lakes, in St. David, Arizona, for two weeks at a time. In addition, CCC allows members to stay in participating "resorts" (fancy word for RV parks) for $1.00 per night. Members can stay a week at each place (per six-month period), which is fine with us, since that's about as long as we'd want to stay anyway. Now we have another big directory, this one listing 500 CCC resorts.

EAST CANYON RESORT, HENEFER, UTAH
August 5-11, 1991

Our first experiment with the CCC system was the place we're staying now. Not only had we never heard of it before, but it appeared to be in the middle of nowhere. Once we found the town of Henefer, we drove about twelve miles south, and suddenly this *beautiful* resort materialized. Besides WIDE grassy RV spaces, the area is surrounded by trees. *And* the park includes a tennis court (!) and two large swimming pools—all well-maintained.

So we've really taken advantage of the resort facilities. As our "next-door" neighbor Jim said, "Do you think you're getting your dollar's worth?" We just keep pinching ourselves. Jim has been a CCC member for eight years, and he said some resorts are better than others; this happens to be one of the nicer ones. We're glad our first impression of CCC traveling is such a good one. I think we can be more philosophical if we're not so lucky next time.

I suppose I should tell you some tales of woe to balance out all this Little-Mary-Sunshine stuff. So, let me see, here's one about our neighbors at Blue Mesa—the grandparents, Loud-Mouth Lola and her hubby; the young parents; a cute baby boy; and a barky dog. I never actually *SAW* the dog; I'm just taking Howard's word for it. Personally, I think they'd bought one of those fake wind-up things at Spencer's.

One day the humanoids went out for the day, leaving Barky to bark. They returned *very late* (midnight?), and began making *strange* noises. I suppose we should have gotten up to investigate, but it was more interesting to speculate. We decided they must have spent their day collecting a million tin cans, and when they came home they had to STIR those cans. And stir and stir and stir.

We also figured that, after coming home so late, they would probably sleep late the next morning. But no, they were up at 6:00 to stir their cans again. Well, I hate to keep you in suspense, but we never discovered how their tin-can project turned out, because we left that same day.

Some things we had to get used to, in the days before the proliferation of cell phones, were the limitations in keeping in touch with family and friends. Using pay phones was always an adventure—especially when it rained. Once we even shared the phone booth with a resident snake. But—hey—it beat smoke signals.

At least our mail-forwarding service worked well. We had our mail sent once a week since we relocated so frequently (and didn't always know where we would be till we actually got there).

BEAR LAKE, IDAHO—August 12-18, 1991

We decided to visit our Zapata friends Dude and Audrey Cain, and are s-l-o-w-l-y making our way to their home in Buhl, Idaho, enjoying the journey as we go.

Although our present campground wasn't on the way to Buhl, it looked only an inch or two out of the way on the map, so we gave it a try. Then Howard remembered we'd driven this way on a long-ago camping trip, so we checked my journal. Almost exactly seven years ago, I had made the following entry:

> Drove by beautiful turquoise Bear Lake near Utah-Idaho-Wyoming border. Lunch in Afton; camped nearby. Hiked; picked wild raspberries. Visited by a moose.

My diary isn't even grammatical, let alone the stuff racy best-selling novels are made of. But reading between the lines brought back fond memories.

I think the moose incident overshadowed everything in my memory bank that day. While Howard was off gathering firewood, I sat at our picnic table writing postcards. I looked up to find an enormous animal, the likes of which I'd never seen before, standing a few feet away. I was practically paralyzed, and he looked a little bewildered himself. Fortunately, he decided not to hang around. I made a beeline for Howard, who said my eyes were as large as saucers. I told him I'd just seen a very ugly deer. Well, he'd seen it too, otherwise I'd have never known it was really a moose.

Bear Lake is even more beautiful than we remembered. And this area claims to be the raspberry capital of the world. In Garden City, five miles south, there's a stand on every corner that advertises "famous" raspberry milkshakes. (Naturally, we had to check one out.) We also bought fresh raspberries and raspberry syrup.

I made an interesting discovery at our campsite. The terrain was a little rugged, and each site had been marked by large boulders (don't ask me why). I'm always trying to learn something, so I watched RVs pull in on either side of us and listened to the conversations between "pilots" (usually husbands) and "copilots" (usually wives). Here's what I learned: Their conversations were identical to Howard's and mine. And I quote:

> Copilots (waving arms, craning necks, and doing knee-bends): "You have *plenty* of room on the passenger side." (pause) "Watch out for that boulder!"

Pilots (slamming on brakes): "What boulder?"

It's reassuring to share these "magic moments" of parking with our fellow travelers.

BANBURY HOT SPRINGS, BUHL, IDAHO
August 19-25, 1991

We finally made it! It's been so much fun getting together with Audrey and Dude. They took us sightseeing, which included a trip to a "Jolly Green Giant" cannery, where we stopped to buy some delicious fresh sweet corn. Buhl lies in the Magic Valley of Idaho, the land of a thousand springs. It's also known as the trout capital of the world. This might make you think Howard caught some trout for dinner, but instead he caught several blue gills (also tasty).

Much to our surprise, our last day here was very quiet. We expected the park to be overrun by people taking one last summer fling, but—happily—we were wrong. Maybe it's because some schools have already started, and/or people are going home to buy new pencils, crayons, and whatnot. But today we had the park all to ourselves.

Well, *almost* all to ourselves. The squirrels decided to reclaim the park now that school is back in session (somehow they got the word). On our way back from a walk yesterday, we saw one nibbling something right outside our front door. The "something" turned out to be Howard's shoe—I guess the lining looked like the stuff of which good nests are made. He (the squirrel, not Howard) scampered up the tree as we approached. I told him he was *not* to make off with any more of our belongings, but he just flattened himself against the tree and pretended not to hear.

Later in the day, some other campers arrived. One family had a little girl about five, and a little boy about a year-and-a-half. The little boy reminded me of my son Mike at that age, with his crew-cut and his walk that's half-swagger, half-waddle.

This morning the daddy and the little girl went off to fish, but "Mikey" had to stay behind with his mother because he wouldn't drink his orange juice. He was sitting at the far side of the picnic table, and all you could *see* were his chubby little legs swinging (under the table) and his baseball cap (above the table). But you could hear a little disembodied voice emanating from the picnic table, calling, "Hi!" to everyone who passed by.

When Audrey and Dude came to tell us goodbye, we sat under a tree and watched the leaves fall (!) The weather was still warm, but the colors were already changing. The other day we heard the tail end of an item on TV about the significance of St. Bartholomew's Day (August 24) regarding the weather. We never did find out what it was all about, but if any of you know if St. Bart saw his shadow or something, and what that might mean, please let us know.

We hear the Canada geese have started south early this year, so we're thinking it might be time for us to do the same.

ON THE ROAD—August 26-29, 1991

The Cains, who are enthusiastic travelers, recommended visiting Kamiah and Coeur d'Alene, two of their favorite Idaho towns. Being the slowpokes that we are, we stopped at a couple of RV parks along the way. To reach the first Resort-slash-RV Park, we had to bump over a mile-long *rough* road to the office, where we discovered that the trailer riff-raff were situated out of view of the "Resort" clientele. Which meant jouncing back down the aforementioned *rough* road, plus lurching another quarter of a mile, to the RV entrance.

The campground was nice enough, seemed fairly new—and evidently unheard-of. Of the eighty sites, only ten were filled. Of those ten, only five (including ours) appeared to be occupied. We saw only one neighbor to wave to. So much for potlucks.

MEADOWS RV PARK, NEW MEADOWS, IDAHO
August 30 through September 2, 1991

Our next stop was a winner, a "mom-and-pop" place, in the woods, small and neighborly. So we were happily situated for the

Labor Day weekend. We walked around town, which reminded us a little of Chama—another to put on our list of favorites. Just north of town is the 45th parallel, halfway between the equator and the North Pole.

A small fair was held at the town square to celebrate the holiday. We'd become friendly with a couple from Arizona, and we all walked over together to join in the cake walk and other festivities.

It was here that I made an enlightening discovery. Among the townspeople was a (one) Black person. I found myself staring at him, and was embarrassed when I caught myself. I realized what seemed so strange was that I hadn't seen anyone of *any* "ethnic group" since coming to Idaho. (Unless you count "palefaces.")

Back home I never even *think* about ethnicity. I hadn't realized how much I take our New Mexican diversity for granted, but now I appreciate it even more.

LEWIS-CLARK RESORT, KAMIAH, IDAHO
September 3-9, 1991

We used to think Kamiah was pronounced to rhyme (kind of) with "Mariah" until the Cains explained that Kamiah is pronounced "kammy-eye." Of course, you already knew that. (Let's hear these Idaho people say "Bernalillo.")

From the Santa Fe Trail to the Lewis and Clark Trail, we've now come about 1200 miles. This is a beautiful part of the country, and we've enjoyed both God-made and man-made local attractions.

This past week we've felt a little closer to the equator than the North Pole. Friday the temp was 95°, which was much *cooler* than I'd have guessed (i.e., it felt closer to 115°). Idaho has been undergoing a severe drought, and it's sad to see things that are usually lush looking so dry. But Monday it finally rained, and Tuesday was cloudy and cool off and on.

Lewis-Clark is another CCC park, and the most accommodating RV park we've ever visited. The park offers daily arts-and-crafts workshops, weekly tours, Bingo, movies, and ** ICE-CREAM SOCIALS **. (Guess which event we attended.)

This resort is situated on the Nez Perce reservation. Right across the street is "The Heart of the Monster," a place sacred to the Nez Perce Indians, a place where the Monster's heart is said to have turned to stone. According to legend, the Monster swallowed up all the inhabitants of the ancient world. After a lengthy journey and eventual battle, Coyote cut the heart out of the "Swallowing Monster" and restored the human race. Coyote then sent the various tribes in different directions. Last of all, he created the Nez Perce, or *Nimíipuu*, from the blood of the Monster. Coyote promised they would be "a people strong and brave, with good hearts."

I find myself wanting to know more and more about Indian history—and the history of every place we visit. I remember the names Lewis and Clark and Sacagawea from school days, but my memory of that era would fill a short paragraph. After spending time here, it seems much more tangible.

We like the town of Kamiah too. (This is where the Nez Perce tribe spent the winters manufacturing "kamia" ropes.) Not only is this town pretty, but everyone is so friendly. When we went in to collect our mail, the postmaster welcomed us and recommended a scenic picnic area and beach called "Three Devils."

We checked it out (to see whether he liked tourists or not—ooooh, that little cynical voice) and were glad we did. The highway follows the aptly named Clearwater River, and the area is heavily forested. There are frequent pullouts designed for gawkers.

On the way back, we sampled some huckleberry pie, which is a local treat. Howard liked it, but I'll stick with raspberry. We also wandered through Kooskia (rhymes with "goose-key"). We find this little town (population about 700) fascinating. There's something sort of surreal about it—almost makes us feel as if we've been transported to another dimension. Kooskia looks (and the name sounds) like something out of the TV series *Northern Exposure*, and we find ourselves on the lookout for Dr. Fleishman, or Ed, or maybe a moose moseying down main street. In fact, Howard swears he's already seen Marilyn Whirlwind there.

Speaking of mail, it's always good to get news from home and news of the grandchildren. We hear that Adrienne isn't sure what to make of kindergarten. She says her teacher collects their papers and puts them in a blue box which Adrienne thinks is going to be mailed off someplace where they'll never be heard of again. Here's Margot's summary of the first day of first grade: "I don't want to talk about it."

Ben isn't happy about starting third grade either. The first night, he reported that he didn't feel good. He said the little girl who sat near him had a bunch of allergies, and he figured he'd caught them all.

Poor kids, I'm afraid they take after their grandmother. I can remember transferring to another school my sophomore year in *college*, and still feeling that lonely new-kid-on-the-block lump in my throat—or was it my stomach? Maybe my toes.

Where to next? We hope to reach the Oregon coast eventually, and from there we'll figure out which desert to cross to get back to Albuquerque.

COEUR D'ALENE, IDAHO
September 10-14, 1991

So many people had told us how lovely Coeur d'Alene is, we decided to check it out for ourselves. We found it all we'd hoped for and more. I'm convinced it should be called "The City Beautiful USA."

A picturesque resort hotel rises above the downtown area. Although simpler in design and relatively new, it has an old-world charm that reminds me of Le Château Frontenac in Québec City. We're not exactly sure where the grounds of the hotel leave off and the City Park begins, but the combined area is *vast* and green and shady, with a profusion of bright red geraniums bordering the walks. The park faces the lake, which is usually dotted by colorful sailboats, paragliders, and small tour-boats—to say nothing of a few hardy ducks.

Since this was out of the way—and meant going north rather than south—we'd cautiously allowed ourselves only five days. Not enough! Ironically, we'd originally been somewhat hesitant about going at all, because we'd read—some years back—that the neo-Nazi "Aryan Nations" made their headquarters nearby. Maybe they thought they could make some inroads in a state of so many "palefaces."

However we also read that the local churches had rallied together and taken a definite stand *against* the Aryan Nations group and their activities. I guess they're at somewhat of an impasse—no one can legally force the Aryan Nations to leave; but it appears they've been effectively prevented from making much headway here, which is encouraging.

From Coeur d'Alene we went to Moses Lake, Washington. That was not one of our better driving days; it was hot, and we missed a couple of turns. The RV park had *very* short spaces, so backing in was tricky. This time, instead of boulders, we had other people's vehicles to avoid. But, after struggling through several zig-zags, we finally got situated.

In general, RVers are more than ready to help one another in any and all situations. Sometimes they can be TOO helpful—several people giving directions at once can be distracting. Still we appreciate the intent. This time was an exception that had us shaking our heads in disbelief. A man who'd been watching the proceedings from across the way waited until we'd ended our struggle, then ambled over and informed Howard, "I could have parked that in one try."

So we were more than ready for a friendly face when we discovered that our next-door neighbors were the very same nice people who'd camped next door to us at Bear Lake. It was almost like running into family.

RANDLE, WASHINGTON
September 16-20, 1991

After our one day at Moses Lake, we came to Randle—the "gateway to Mt. St. Helens." We'd scheduled only three days there, thinking it might be somewhat desolate due to the volcano's eruption a few years ago. Even on the map, the area looks white and dreary. Get out a magnifying glass and look for Randle!

As we drove up the mountain toward Mt. St. Helens, we were startled at the abrupt change in terrain. One minute we were surrounded by lush green evergreens. Then, as if we'd crossed an imaginary boundary, we found ourselves in the midst of a stark gray landscape, reminiscent of pictures the astronauts sent back from their moon landing. However, as we looked closer, we saw signs of nature's resiliency—small green seedlings, bright pink fireweed, and cheerful wildflowers cropping up here and there.

In marked contrast to the devastation at Mt. St. Helens, we saw thick forests all around Washington. We stayed in Randle longer than planned so we could go to Mt. Rainier *and* have time just to enjoy our surroundings.

Our "surroundings" included blackberry bushes, which we found irresistible. While growing up in Houston, I used to go "berryin'" (which is short for "berry-pickin'") every summer with a couple of other kids. I'd bring my berries back to Aunt Leah Belle, who'd make pies and cobblers.

So berryin' this trip was not only fun, but also nostalgic. Did I mention challenging? The biggest, juiciest berries were always deep within the vines, almost blanketed by the sprawling webs of big hairy spiders guarding their domain. Still, we picked enough berries for Howard to enjoy them on his breakfast cereal for several days.

I used to be pretty fatalistic about the idea of moving away from earthquake-prone areas and the like. I mean, if one disaster doesn't get you, another one probably will, so it always seems a trade-off. But Mount St. Helens made a believer of me. Earthquake here, folks? Volcano? Say no more—I'll just be moseying on, thank you.

It was interesting to talk to people who'd been in Randle when the volcano erupted. The girl in the gift shop said it stayed dark for three hours, the air so thick with ash she couldn't even see a lamp in front of her. It sounded terrifyingly claustrophobic. If you *knew* it would be over at a set time (like three hours), it would be one thing; but to wonder when it would end—and what the end would be—I can't imagine!

You're not supposed to remove anything from the area, but Howard and I suspected if we vacuumed our clothes and truck afterward, we could probably fill hundreds of little plastic sandwich bags with enough ash to sell as souvenirs.

OCEAN CITY, WASHINGTON
September 21-26, 1991

Time has been zipping by, and while we aren't exactly zipping with it, we haven't been sitting still either.

We'd discovered how scenic Highway 12 is near Randle, and we'd heard it's a gorgeous drive from Kamiah clear to Missoula eastward. We began to wonder if it would be just as scenic going west. So westward we went.

Highway 12 ends (or begins, depending) at Aberdeen Washington, and just beyond that is Ocean City. We took long walks while we were there, looking for treasure along the beaches. The beaches were quite clean however. This is *not* a complaint! No, we did not miss the aluminum cans, plastic rings, Styrofoam doodads, etc. But there weren't many shells. Maybe this explains why the sand was so smooth, which made walking a pleasure. We did find lots of sand dollars on nearby Copalis Beach. (Looking for those can become as addictive as berryin'.)

We also found a number of crab claws that Howard thought we could bleach and hang all over our trailer. He thinks of everything.

I love to watch the comical little sandpipers! They skitter down to the waterline, then skitter back pell-mell as soon as the waves reach their toes, their skinny little legs whirring like egg-beaters. They always seem so surprised to discover the waves are wet. Over and over—each time amazed.

We enjoy watching the gulls too. Every now and then, you can see several of them lined up along the shore like sentinels, and you'd swear they'd *placed* themselves at the exact same distance from one another.

OREGON TRAVELS
September 27 through October 17, 1991

I don't know when the "early winter" that was predicted last month is supposed to come crashing in on us, but so far we've been enjoying "unseasonably warm" weather. If I wait for the weather to turn bad—or the scenery ugly—before I write again, who knows when that will be?

From Ocean City, Washington, we went to Seaside, Oregon. It seemed appropriate for us to stop there, since that was the end of the Lewis-Clark trail we'd been following off and on. We arrived the weekend of Oktoberfest, so lots of things were going on, including a parade that was just our style: About half a block long, it consisted of a couple of oom-pah-pah bands, with people dressed in Bavarian-type costumes, and a few clowns. The whole parade put everyone in a festive mood. What fun!

That evening we took a sentimental journey to Oceanside. Three years ago, we'd gone there almost by accident. Back then, we were driving *north* along the coast to Tillamook, but found no room at the inn. We saw a motel ("The House on the Hill") advertised in Oceanside, nine miles west, and headed that way. It was twilight, the atmosphere eerie and foggy, the road lined with dense evergreens. I began feeling more and more apprehensive, wondering if this motel might be one in a chain owned by Norman Bates of *Psycho* fame.

The manager was on the roof when we arrived, but he came down to greet us in his bright-red long-sleeved undershirt and denim overalls. Not exactly the Waldorf-Astoria—but not Norman's place either! The room turned out to be cozy and attractive, with a view of the ocean from the "hill" (translate, "cliff").

Next, we asked the manager if he could suggest someplace to go for supper. He pointed down the cliff and said, "Well, there's Roseanna's down there." I couldn't see much of anything, but we thanked him and wound our way to the main street again.

Roseanna's was rather plain from the outside, but what a treat was in store for us. Not only was the meal excellent, but all the tables were arranged so diners could view the ocean. Someone played soft music on the piano, and flowers graced each table. Altogether it was a wonderful romantic place.

They say you can't go back, but in this case, that wasn't so. We couldn't see any changes in the town *or* Roseanna's, and our visit this time was just as happy as the last.

*   *   *

In Coos Bay we visited the National Wildlife Refuge on Cape Arago, where we watched (and listened to) hundreds of sea lions on the rocks nearby. We used our binoculars to see them clearly, but hearing them was no problem. We heard their loud barking the minute we got out of the truck. Later, when we visited a botanical garden a few miles up the road, the sea lions were out of sight, but still not out of sound.

From Coos Bay we went to Brookings for a few days. This is the southernmost town in Oregon on Hwy. 101, and our last stay on the coast. We had driven down the entire coastal highway of Oregon, and noticed a state park every few miles. It makes the coast seem like one long park, and we're grateful that so much beauty has been preserved for everyone to enjoy.

From Brookings we drove eastward to Talent. During our stay there, we visited Ashland, seven miles away, the home of Oregon's summer Shakespeare Festival. It's a pretty town filled with Victorian homes. I don't think those are Shakespearean; still they seemed to offer the right ambiance.

I was wearing my "New Mexico" T-shirt, which caught the attention of an elderly gentleman who'd lived in Raton at one time. He seemed pleasant and offered to show us some of the sights. As it turned out, he had an ax to grind, and the *sight* he wanted to show us was the *site* where he'd picketed somebody.

He also took us a block off the beaten track so we could look at some hippies. I felt very odd "looking at" anyone, and hardly in a position to frown on anyone else's appearance, being the fashion plate that I am in my T-shirt and tennies. Actually, everyone in that town dressed a little oddly, so I fit right in. I saw several people (probably Festival participants) running around in 16th-century outfits, and no one paid any attention.

This region is situated in the "Rogue Valley"—with the Rogue River running through it—and I got a kick out of seeing various institutions named for the area; for example, the Rogue Bank. Doesn't sound like a place you'd want to park your life savings, does it! My favorite was "Rogue Opportunity Center." (Job openings for rogues?)

There's also a Rogue Community College.

"Are you a college graduate?"

"No, but I'm a Rogue scholar."

Incidentally, we've had fun with signs we've seen along the way. One place advertised "Hot Dogs and Night Crawlers." (You can stop inserting "beautiful" now.) We'd hate for someone to get careless while fixing our hot dog. The fish probably feel the same way about the bait.

One of our favorites throughout Idaho was "Watch for Rock." They never specified *which* rock to be on the lookout for, and there were so many to choose from! Hope we didn't miss out on some kind of reward.

HOME IS WHERE YOU PARK IT
October 24, 1991

We're finally on the way to Albuquerque. I started to say we're heading *homeward*, but we're trying to broaden our idea of "home." At this point we're a mere 950 miles, more or less, from Albuquerque, a place where we like to visit family and friends.

We're parked outside Yosemite National Park, which we explored yesterday. Some people are still camped there—in tents—and we're happy to leave the roughing it to the youngsters. A cold front came through the other night, and it's nice to be indoors today (*and* to have our electric blanket).

Before coming here, we stopped at a CCC park in Smith, Nevada, which is in the middle of nowhere, but also quiet and peaceful. Sunday we decided to go to church, but it turned out that all the churches in town were holding an auction and had canceled their regular services. So what was left to do but gamble? (When in Nevada . . . .)

About 25 miles from Smith is the town of Yerington, where we wasted the afternoon inside a dark smoky casino pouring our laundry change into a couple of very hungry machines. So what if we don't wear clean clothes next week?

December 1991

We're spending the Christmas holidays in Phoenix. Our granddaughters Margot, age six, and Adrienne, age five, are really a pair! One afternoon Howard took them to the park where they could play while he hit tennis balls against the backboard. When he was ready to leave, they were dilly-dallying around, so he told them he was going to collect the balls, then meet them at the car.

WELL, I guess they thought he was going to leave without them. So in their hurry to catch up, Adrienne tripped and stubbed her toe. Margot picked her up and carried her piggy-back to the car. Howard was unaware of all the commotion till they reached him. But when they got back home, Margot came in full of righteous indignation to tell my daughter Linda some melodramatic tale of how Adrienne had had a crippling accident from which she, Margot, had single-handedly rescued her, while "Grandpa just ack-nored us!"

While poking through boxes looking for old photos at my folks' house, I happened to discover a collection of letters written by my grandfather from France during "THE" World War (WWI). Sometime after returning home, he gathered all the handwritten letters he'd sent his family and typed them into manuscript form.

He'd also included a prologue saying he hoped these letters might someday be interesting to his *grandchildren*. It gave me the strangest feeling—as if I'd gotten a personal letter from him! I barely remember my grandfather. All my grandparents died while I was quite young. But reading his letters made me feel close to him. He loved France, the French people, the French language. The one week I spent in France I felt drawn to it too. I wish I could have talked with him about our experiences there.

The paper in his manuscript is fragile, the typing pale, so I plan to retype it and send clean copies to the other grandchildren.

I'm including an excerpt here from a letter he wrote to his daughter (my aunt) Marjorie:

NOVEMBER 8, 1917—*The concierge has a little girl 2-1/2 years old that looks like you. She is round and chubby and has blue eyes and yellow hair. Her name is Jeanne Tiercelin. She jabbers at me in French, but she can't talk plain, so I can't understand her. I can't understand French unless it is plain and slow. So I give her a piece of chocolate candy and she smiles and we understand that very well.*

*   *   *

We enjoyed the excitement of the children at Christmastime. Margot and Adrienne got "Sparkle" dolls—something six-year-old Margot said "I've wanted all my life." So the year ended with happy memories to build on.

1992

ZAPATA, TEXAS
January 14 through March 31, 1992

January 16, 1992

It's been raining/*SNOWING* all day long. Since snow is so unusual in this part of Texas, we began to wonder if our weather-luck ran out, or if we'd become snow magnets, or what! We raced a blizzard into Albuquerque on Halloween and experienced a severe storm the day we left Tempe, Arizona, the beginning of January. Our one day in St. David, Arizona, was rainy and dreary. The brief time we were in El Paso, Texas, we drove across town through windy snow/slush.

While in El Paso we visited our friend Liz Fulton and her 90-year-old mother. Mamacita has some interesting stories to tell about her childhood in Parral, Mexico. She was twelve years old when Pancho Villa raided her village. She remembers how the villagers tried to keep the women safe by telling the soldiers there was smallpox in the home. She has a hard time understanding why there's a state park in New Mexico *honoring* Pancho Villa.

When we finally arrived in Zapata, Sonia, the manager of the RV park, had saved us a spot that is just as nice as the one we had before. From our living room we have a beautiful view of the lake and the bridge into town. We can watch water birds during the day and sunsets in the evening.

At the moment, of course, everything looks like a gray blob, but WE KNOW THAT SCENERY IS OUT THERE! We also have a large mesquite tree at the edge of our yard, which—likewise—we don't need at the moment, but SOMEDAY WE WILL WELCOME THE SHADE!

January 24, 1992

Even when it's rainy, Zapata has a magical effect on us. Much as we still look forward to traveling, a part of us is in no hurry to leave. Howard began talking about coming back here from the moment we left last year. But last summer when we visited the Cains, I told Audrey I was almost afraid to come back because we'd loved it so much before. What if it had changed?

She said, "Don't worry. It'll be the same—you'll see."

She's right: It's still wonderful.

It's so nice to switch gears from "big-city" living. One example of the small-town atmosphere: You never know whether the post office and some of the stores are going to be open or not, because the lone person running wherever-it-is-you-want-to-go takes off at odd hours for lunch.

Dude Cain recommended a CPA, Eddie Martínez, to do our taxes; and when Dude explained how to get to Eddie's office, he said, "It's six blocks north of the traffic light."

"*The*" traffic light! Actually, this town could use a couple more, but that's beside the point.

It also seems strange to hear about "the" Catholic Church, or "the" Methodist Church, or "the" Lutheran Church. They all have names, of course, but since there's only one of each, they're usually referred to as "the."

The downside of living here: No bagels, no Häagen-Dazs ice-cream bars. AND the mud—after a rain—is mixed with clay-like caliche. In fact, I suspect there's caliche in the drinking water, which might eventually lead to hardening of the brain. That's my excuse anyway.

January 31, 1992

We're finally seeing some sunshine (at least, that's what the man on the radio told us "that yellow spot" is). Just in time: We were beginning to look around for ark-building instructions.

The weather was lovely this afternoon (about 75°), and we almost felt guilty being so lazy. Then we decided God wouldn't have made folding chairs if He hadn't wanted people to stretch out and enjoy looking at His lake and water birds.

There is no movie theater in Zapata, but I doubt that movies could be any more entertaining than watching the pelicans and egrets around here. Besides being rather comical-looking, the pelicans are *huge*. From a distance they look like the big inflatable toys kids ride in the swimming pool. When they fly, their wing-span is so wide, they look like hang-gliders.

It's also funny to watch the snowy egrets land in the feathery (and obviously very flexible) mesquite tree in our back yard at the edge of the lake. Whenever one of those enormous white birds plops down in the highest branches, it seems as out of place as if a St. Bernard had perched there.

The fishermen in our RV park have named one egret "Freddy the Freeloader," because he hangs around the area where they clean fish, as if the scraps were his due.

One Sunday I asked Howard to come to Mass with me because there was going to be a special service honoring the Quinceañeras. Well, the priest mumbled something about things not getting organized, and the front pew reserved for the honorees remained vacant. (But we thought we spotted a few fifteen-year-olds all dressed up, scattered here and there.) Then at the end of the Mass, he mumbled something about donating money for the parking-lot fund: "Give a dollar, five, a million, whatever."

He also said he hadn't gotten around to typing up the financial statement, but everything was OK, and he gave a few figures. The week before, he said he was supposed to read a letter from the Bishop, but he'd lost it. But he knew what it said.

To give credit where it's due, I have no doubts about his faith and integrity. He just can't be bothered with what he considers administrative minutiae.

March 25, 1992

The beginning of this month, I flew to Phoenix for a few days for my folks' 60th anniversary celebration. The Laredo International

Airport is much smaller than its title suggests. It serves five commuter-type airlines, three of them serving Mexico, plus the American Eagle (into/out of Dallas), and the Continental Express (into/out of Houston).

For my flight out, we got to the airport at 5:40, the customary one hour early, then discovered the counter didn't even open till 6:00. When it did open, there were two ticket agents. After they'd finished checking everyone in, one of them went out to load baggage, while the other one took us through a security check and collected our tickets. Everything went smoothly—it was just a new experience.

Actually, I like flying those smaller planes—you don't have to wait so long for your ginger ale. On the return trip, the flight attendant was having a problem with the P.A., so she just *told* us our instructions.

In both Arizona and South Texas, the huisache was in full bloom, the leaves filling out with yellow-orange fuzzy balls, about the size of small marbles. From a distance, it looks like a golden haze, which is especially pretty near green trees. It has the most wonderful distinctive fragrance. When I got off the plane in Laredo, that was the first thing I noticed, and it was like a friendly "welcome home." So with Howard and the huisache both there to greet me, it was good to be back. And *home* has truly become Zapata now— at least we consider it our *winter* home, although we travel the country the rest of the year.

A parade kicked off the Zapata County Fair the 14th, and the whole town turned out. We lined our pickups along the main street two hours early so we could get good seats from our tailgates.

Both the high-school and mid-school bands were impressive, and there were a number of elaborate floats. My favorite was one promoting ecology, entered by a first-grade classroom. They had painted some old tires green and stacked them up in varying sizes to build a gigantic realistically shaped dinosaur. In addition to that, the children had made flowers out of plastic and cans— colorful and creative.

On St. Patrick's Day, we went with a group of seventeen people to Corpus Christi to see "Los Barcos" (the replicas of the ships Columbus sailed). The replicas are the exact size as the original ships, and it's hard to imagine anyone crossing the Atlantic in those tiny boats!

The weather was rather inconsistent all last week. One day it got up to 94° in the shade (hmmmm, I don't hear any sighs of envy). The next day was relatively cold (65°)—or relatively warm, depending on your location; we heard it snowed in New York the same day.

Today we took a day trip with Dorothy and Doyle Skinner, exploring both sides of the US-Mexican border south of Zapata. One of the most unusual off-the-beaten-path adventures was taking the Los Ebanos ferry across a narrow stretch of the Rio Grande, a few miles west of McAllen. This is the only hand-drawn ferry in existence on either side of the border, and carries no more than three cars at a time. We opted to go on foot, and Howard and Doyle were allowed to assist the crew and other passengers in pulling the ropes that transported the ferry.

The closest town on the Mexican side, Ciudad Díaz Ordaz, was two miles away, so we decided to turn around and ferry back to Los Ebanos rather than walk into town.

The first of April, we plan to move on, following the coastal bend. Then we'll go as far as Biloxi or Pensacola before heading northward. The only "hitch" is that some cactus wrens have built a nest in our "hitch," so we'll have to find a good place to move them first. (The spiders are on their own—we're not relocating any webs!) It's tempting to follow the birds' example and nest here in Zapata, but we're also looking forward to whatever awaits us around the bend.

ROCKPORT, TEXAS—April 4-7, 1992

We spent a week here, just north of Corpus Christi, having fun despite the rain. In fact, one rainy afternoon I taught Howard to play canasta. He'd led me to believe he wasn't very good at cards, but the opposite is true: He has excellent card sense, and I might go so far as to say he's become quite a card shark. We play nearly every day now, and he usually wins.

In between my card-trouncings, we did a lot of puddle-jumping and sightseeing. One of our biggest treats was visiting the nearby Aransas National Wildlife Preserve. We'd no sooner entered the area when an armadillo crossed the street in front of us! Neither of us had ever seen an armadillo (or even an ex-armadillo) before, so we jumped out of the car to take its picture. Naturally it scooted away with some of its buddies, but we saw several more along the trail before the day was over.

In fact, I'll give you our wildlife count: armadillos, javelina, and waterbirds too numerous to count; ten alligators; a couple of whooping cranes; one raccoon; and—last but not least—two large dogs with their Neanderthal owners. We'd stopped in a picnic area to see the javelina up close, but the dogs spooked them away. It puzzled us that anyone would allow their pets to scare away the wildlife they'd supposedly come all the way to the wildlife habitat to observe.

One day we visited "The Big Tree" on Goose Island. Now you must be wondering how we could bear the excitement of visiting a tree. But this wasn't any ordinary tree. It's an enormous live oak bearing an inscription on a stone plaque, written as if told by the tree itself.

Among other things, it told us, "I have seen spring return more than a thousand times. I can remember hundreds of hurricanes, most I'd rather forget; but I withstood."

The Texas Department of Transportation provides free twenty-four hour service on its twenty-car ferries across Corpus Christi Channel. So one sunny day we ferried over to Port Aransas, and from there drove to Mustang Island, where we enjoyed walking along the beach and laughing with the gulls. On the way home, we saw a beauty salon that advertised "Island Hair," and I decided this was just what I needed for summer weather. Don't ask me to describe it; I'll just say the bones give it real class.

ABITA SPRINGS, LOUISIANA
HOME OF MORE ALLIGATORS
April 15-19, 1992

We've played our daily card game, so now's the time for this week's eagerly awaited "Campsite Report." Our campground has lakes on three sides, lots of trees, thick wild honeysuckle, greenery, friendly neighbors, some ducks, and—except for a few grouchy geese—generally peaceful surroundings.

However, there's a weird side to this place too. When we arrived Wednesday, we were met at the gate by Norman—Stormin' Norman as one of the other RVers calls him (or "Stawmin Nawmin" as it's pronounced in Louisiana). Norman is nice, but takes his guard job quite seriously—braving the rain every hour to re-check all the license plates, although this is a very small park and it would be hard for anyone to slip in unobserved.

We were told to park "over there." "Over There" was a circle of maybe twenty sites, none of which was clearly marked—or even unclearly marked; i.e., they were UNmarked. So everyone parked in haphazard fashion and hooked up to whatever water and electricity seemed reasonably close.

They're in the process of building on to the clubhouse, upgrading the sites, etc. The swimming pool and Jacuzzi are presumably finished—at least you see people around the pool. The area is very attractive, pool and Jacuzzi sparkling clean, the water in the Jacuzzi swirling merrily—oh how good that would feel after a day of traveling! Have you ever heard of a cold hot-tub?

Friday it turned stormy, but when the rain let up for a few seconds, we assumed the storm was over and optimistically ran to town to do laundry. By the time we got to the Laundromat, the electricity had gone out, and the rain was coming down in torrents.

When we got back to the RV park, we needed a gondola to get from truck to home, but didn't see one nearby, so we just waded over. Well, Nawmin was still roamin' about with his umbrella and clipboard, so at least we were safe.

The next night a group of people asked us to join them for a crawfish cookout and singalong. We had fun sitting around the campfire singing Hank Williams tunes and other old favorites. From here on out, I'll know there's only one way to sing *When the Saints Go Mahchin' In.*

ON THE ROAD—April 25 through May 3, 1992

Just in case you're sitting around wondering where we are right now, here's an easy way to spot us: Watch the weather news on TV; look for the picture with the big raindrops, and that's where we'll be. Two days after outwaiting the storm in Abita Springs, we had to outwait a tornado before traveling on. But once we reached Pass Christian, Mississippi, the weather was kind to us, and we thoroughly enjoyed our stay in beautiful Mississippi.

Even the interstates take you through miles and miles of woods and greenery (a lovely sight for us desert folk). The major highways, especially through the larger cities, have been excellent, and the rest areas look like parks.

Sometimes the byways leave a little to be desired. We were spoiled in Texas, I guess—even the Farm-to-Market roads are standard width, and well-paved. Some of the so-called two-lane highways we traveled in Louisiana seemed to actually be about a lane-and-a-half wide. There were several signs that read, "Substandard Road." We figured whoever manufactured the signs has probably made his millions and retired by now.

I digress. If you look on a map—a regular one, not the weather one—you'll see Bay St. Louis, Mississippi, on US Highway 90 near the eastern border of Louisiana. From there through Pass Christian and into Gulfport is one of the prettiest routes we've encountered along the coast. On the south side of the highway is the Gulf of Mexico; on the north are impressive mansions on huge lawns complete with honeysuckle and other flowering shrubbery, magnolia trees, and live oaks draped with Spanish moss. Perfect place to take walks.

Up till now, I've had a rather vague impression that Mississippi and other parts of the south were largely populated by racists with limited mental capacity (due to their brains getting smushed by their pointy white hats). Well, it seems *I'm* the one who needs to expand my mind. The places we visited seemed cosmopolitan and progressive, the people friendly and "normal."

From Mississippi we drove through Alabama to Pensacola, Florida. For a change we didn't get rained on, but it was very windy, and *cold.* On the day it reached 104° in Phoenix, we were shivering in a record-breaking cold spell in southern Alabama and the Florida panhandle. We keep packing away our heater and dragging it out again. I *never* pack away sweatshirts.

PIGEON FORGE, TENNESSEE—May 4-12, 1992

Now we're at the "Gateway to the Smokies," where we plan to stay for a week. Good thing we're not in a hurry, because we're due more rain. Actually it's nice to have an excuse to kick back and putter around home.

One day we rode Molly the Trolley into town for 25¢. This is a picturesque town, with a mill by a stream, lots of trees, and quaint little shops. We found a music shop that sold instruments popular in Appalachia, and Howard got interested in playing a dulcimer. He slept on the idea, then went into town and bought one (along with the instruction books that go with it). It's a perfect rainy-day activity (enough said), and he can already play *Aunt Rhody* and *Frère Jacques.* Next step, he says, is acoustics and a big speaker.

We had the most wonderful visits with my cousin Emma Lee Martin and her husband, Ray, who live in Maryville, not far from here. They made us feel so at home and went out of their way to give us a personal tour of the Smokies, showing us their favorite coves and picnic places.

The Martins are semi-retired. Ray has "Maryville's oldest barber shop," which was owned by his father before him, and Emma Lee still does part-time accounting for long-time clients.

Ray and their son Eddie are musicians. (I think everyone in Tennessee is a musician.) One evening when they and another musician played at a retirement home, they invited us to come along. Ray plays a steel guitar, while Eddie and Lawrence each play other types of guitars. What a wonderful concert!

Before World War II put a halt to his career, Ray played professionally as a member of Patsy Montana's band. We'd never heard of Patsy Montana, but found out that, with her recording of *I Want to be a Cowboy's Sweetheart*, she was the first female country-western singer ever to make a "million-copy" hit record.

Monday night Howard and I watched the Country Music Hall of Fame on TV. They honored Patsy Montana, and we actually knew who they were talking about! (Several years later, when Lee Ann Rimes recorded *I Want to be a Cowboy's Sweetheart*, she made it a point to pay tribute to this remarkable lady.)

The next day we stopped at a small gallery where we enjoyed talking with the owner, who uses an atlas to keep track of customers who come from far and near.

"Oh, I've never had anyone here from Mexico before," she told us, but she knew Albuquerque was in the US, promptly found it on her map, and highlighted it in yellow.

When we said it's really "*New*" Mexico, she nodded and continued to call it Mexico. She asked if our kids all had to learn Spanish in school. (What say, kids?)

I've come to realize that other people's ideas about New Mexico are no less strange than my ideas about *their* states. Here's a good test: Say these names and see what pictures come to mind: Hawaii, Alaska, New Jersey, Mississippi, Kansas, Iowa, Texas, Tennessee, California, North Dakota.

Tennessee people, for example, are sometimes thought to be hillbillies and moonshiners who marry their relatives at an early age (which automatically makes every Tennessean related to every other Tennessean). While we were there, Howard kept teasing me about "my people," since I have Tennessee ancestors on both sides of my family tree. Every time we saw someone who looked kind of odd, he'd say, "One of yours?"

Everybody (but us) *talks* so funny. While we were driving through the Smokies with the Martins, Emma Lee told us that on their last trip they'd seen several black buyers. We didn't get the drift till she told us about seeing "a mother buyer and her two cubs." Turnabout: The art-gallery owner said they enjoy hearing strangers pronounce the names of their towns. People who don't know any better say "Maryville," instead of "Murvull."

Must tell another "Where in the world is New Mexico?" story. When someone else east of the Mississippi heard we were from New Mexico, he asked Howard, "How is everything down in Costa Rica?"

RAPHINE, VIRGINIA—May 17, 1992

On our way to Front Royal, we broke up our 330-mile journey by stopping at a dot on the map called "Raphine." We followed the directions in our Campground Directory to a place I'll call "Sycamore Groves." We did well till the last quarter of a mile. Then we turned at a sign that said "Sycamore Groves *Mobile Homes*," instead of "Sycamore Groves *Campground*."

It so happened that a very amiable elderly man drove by and offered to help us out. We followed this nice man, whoever he was, from the mobile home area right into the campground area and right into an RV site.

The RV park was somewhat haphazard, which is beginning to seem standard. The sites were rather overgrown and oddly marked, so I'm not sure we'd have recognized them as such without our guide's help. There were only three or four other RVs, in a place that could have held 100.

Our guide explained that lots of people got confused and turned at the wrong place, so he'd made a sign to clarify things, but somehow he'd never gotten around to putting it up. Howard asked where we should go to pay, and he said just to pay him.

By then it seemed perfectly natural to hand over our $12.00 to a complete stranger and not bother with any kind of paperwork, such as a receipt. It crossed our minds that the "real" owner might show up later and want a "real" payment; then we decided it was unlikely something that logical would happen.

We were by a lake in the woods. And with so few neighbors, it was quiet and serene, a pleasant stay after all.

Unfortunately, we'd had a freak mishap earlier in the day. We'd stopped for lunch at a rest area, and were browsing through our pantry when we felt (and heard) the most awful jolt. We started swaying back and forth and nearly lost our balance—as if we were experiencing an earthquake.

We hurried outside and discovered that—although there was plenty of room between us—the semi parked in front of us had backed into us before pulling out, then had taken off without a backward glance.

People came running over to see if we were all right. Another trucker jumped into his own truck and tried to reach the semi on the CB but got no answer. This guy was pretty disgusted that the trucker who hit us had run away, because he had to have felt the impact. He (the Good Samaritan) stayed with us till the police arrived. The only damage, as it turned out, was to our front bumper—hurray for heavy-duty bumpers. The State Police tracked the driver down in no time, and everything was eventually resolved.

I can certainly think of a thousand things to be grateful for. I don't dwell on awful things that could happen while we're rolling down the highway, so it never occurred to me to worry about what could happen while we weren't moving at all! I think there's a lesson here somewhere.

MEMORIAL DAY WEEKEND—May 22-25, 1992

For a couple of folks who believe in leisurely retirement, we've been doing a lot of dashing around lately. We spent the holiday weekend *Not Sightseeing*. Instead we sat it out in the George Washington National Forest at Elizabeth Furnace Campground, just south of Waterlick, Virginia. I don't know where they come up with these names—probably something very famous that I'm too uninformed to know about. Well, yes, I *have* heard of George

Washington . . . We discovered that the lovely greenery surrounding our campsite was poison ivy, so we stepped gingerly. The campground itself was somewhat remote, so we were far from the madding crowd during the madding weekend.

PENNSYLVANIA—May 26 through June 22, 1992

A few weeks ago, we hadn't given much thought to Pennsylvania. It was just someplace to travel through to get to New York to visit my sister and her fiancé. Surprise! By the time we leave Pennsylvania, we will have spent four weeks here.

It began when we thought, since it's on the way, let's visit Gettysburg. I had no idea this would turn out to be such an emotional experience. What a paradox this place is. The peaceful idyllic countryside punctuated by somber war memorials at every turn. Seminary Ridge, Peach Orchard, Plum Run, and Wheatfield alongside Cemetery Ridge, Devil's Den, Bloody Run, and Valley of Death. Lincoln's "few appropriate remarks" that he thought "the world will little note nor long remember . . . ."

Another thing that impressed me was the tragedy of Americans at war against other Americans. The blood-filled rivers didn't differentiate between blue-uniformed Americans or gray-uniformed Americans.

What I found most moving was the Eternal Peace Monument, where the emphasis was on healing our differences. The inscription reads, "Peace Eternal in a Nation United." When President Roosevelt dedicated the monument in 1938—seventy-five years after the battle of Gettysburg—the statistics say that "there were veterans of both wars present . . . whose average age was 94." This really caught my attention.

Living to be 94 is pretty remarkable in itself, but I got to thinking: Seventy-five years ago, if their *average* age was 19, how much younger some of them actually must have been . . . . Young, homesick, disenchanted . . . . Even more remarkable, although they had been involved in the war on opposite sides, these boys-grown-into-men had come together as friends to focus on peace!

From Gettysburg we went to the Pennsylvania Dutch area, home of religious people who've given their towns rather startling names: Blue Ball (where we found a restaurant with an excellent smorgasbord), Bird-in-Hand, Paradise, and Intercourse. Is it too indelicate to say we found Intercourse delightful? Our favorite of these four towns, it seemed to attract a mixture of townspeople and tourists, so we didn't feel we were simply in an artificial tourist trap.

While there, we saw a short documentary film on the Amish and Mennonites, and came away feeling that we are much more alike than different—in goals and ideals anyway. The Amish, I learned, are not anti-electricity per se; they just avoid whatever they perceive would distract them from their God and their families.

The more we travel, the more we've become aware that there's hardly any place, event, or culture that someone hasn't figured out how to make big bucks on. This hasn't stopped me from liking T-shirts and souvenirs, but I've gotten less susceptible to the sales-pitch.

Thank goodness they haven't made a theme park out of Gettysburg. We did appreciate the $10.00 bus tour we took. We skipped a lot of other places that might have been interesting but became collectively expensive. We didn't feel like paying $3.75 apiece, for example, to see a door a bullet had gone through.

Similarly, when we were among the Amish people, we skipped the $18.95-per-person tour to drive by their farms and stare at them (when we could drive by and stare for free). Actually, we tried to be as unobtrusive as possible, but it would have been impossible not to be curious about such a different way of life.

In one store, Howard noticed the teen-age Amish girl behind the counter and the teen-age daughter of a tourist/customer eyeing each other with a mixture of reticence and curiosity. He said their expressions were identical, as if to say, "What is it like to live in your world?"

It was fascinating to see so many horse-and-buggies, all with modern bright orange triangular warning signs on the back. The farmhouses were large and surprisingly attractive. Outside were long, long clotheslines, with rows and rows of black pants and jackets on them, as well as pastel shirts and dresses. Children were dressed like miniature adults: the little girls in plain dresses with dark pinafores and bonnets, the little boys in dark suits with light-colored straw hats.

Hershey, Pennsylvania, "The Sweetest Place on Earth," is as enticing as it sounds, and an ideal place for a theme park. We chose the trolley ride instead, and enjoyed our conductors who entertained us while educating us on our tour of the town.

We learned that Milton Hershey was much more than a hugely successful entrepreneur and candymaker. A man of deep integrity, he felt a commitment to extend his good fortune to others. Around 1900, on the grounds of his parents' original farm, he built an entire town for his family and employees. He wasn't satisfied with building mere "living quarters," but hired architects to design unique and attractive homes for every family. Eventually the town included schools, parks, a zoo, a theater, and businesses essential to the community. The two main streets intersect at Chocolate Avenue and Cocoa Avenue. Streetlamps are shaped like giant Hershey kisses.

From Hershey we went to Scotrun, where we had perfect weather. It was the first full week since mid-March without any rainy—or even cloudy—days. Scotrun is right in the middle of the Poconos, less than seven miles from Camelback ski area, which we could see across the lake from us. Easterners and Westerners have different ideas on what constitutes a mountain, but we must confess theirs are beautiful, however short, completely covered with trees and other greenery.

Lake Adventure Campground near Milford borders a 76,000-acre game preserve. Although it's a treat to see deer in the woods, it's a little unsettling to see them cross the highway in broad daylight.

One morning while doing my exercises, I looked out the window and found myself face-to-face with a deer! Or rather, face-to-window. Our windows are reflective, and I wondered if the deer thought it was looking at another deer, or if it was simply amazed to find me doing something so energetic so early in the morning.

CROTON POINT PARK, NEW YORK
June 23 through July 8, 1992

We enjoyed a two-week visit with my sister and her fiancé, Louise and Bill. They live in Ossining, only a few miles south of our campground.

Since we were so close to New York City, Howard and I decided to spend a day there and visit Ellis Island. We caught the commuter train at Ossining (easy), got off at Grand Central Station (easy—it's the last stop), then searched for the right bus to take us to "the Battery" (insane). We were looking for the "102" bus, but not all "102" buses go to the same destination, for some reason known only to the New York transit system. So we stopped every "102" bus that came along till we found the right one. Our driver was very patient, and didn't even mind that we asked him ten times where we were supposed to get off.

As we walked the last few blocks toward the ferry, we began feeling a little overwhelmed by the sheer numbers of people, all going in different directions. Too late we realized we should have strapped ourselves together with a sturdy bungee cord, just in case we got separated. And of course we had to make our way around the police roadblocks set up for the protest du jour.

We found New York City people to be friendly and helpful, contrary to stereotype. They were unfailingly pleasant about answering our questions. ("Where are we? How do we get someplace else?")

While waiting for the ferry, a young Japanese-American couple from California asked me for directions. *Moi!* So after sharing a laugh over the fact that anyone would mistake me for a person who might actually *know* something, and discovering that we were practically neighbors (all being from west of the Mississippi), we soon felt like old friends.

Meanwhile, there were some self-styled street acrobats entertaining the waiting crowd with their antics. One of them began picking volunteers from the crowd to participate in one of his stunts. He lined up five people, then took a flying leap over them all, as the rest of us watched, entranced. One of the people he picked was our new-found friend, whose wife videotaped the whole thing. What an adventure *they'll* have to remember.

Ellis Island was fascinating. Not only viewing the exhibits, but actually being in the buildings where so many immigrants—including Howard's ancestors—began their lives in this country was a memorable experience. We found a wall that listed several Tesslers, but none that we recognized. The list is incomplete because only those names volunteered by present-day family members are included.

We went back to Grand Central via subway. People were actually chatting with friends and *laughing* on the subway. No one got violent, or even mildly rude.

LAKE GEORGE, NEW YORK—July 9-22, 1992

Our stay with Louise and Bill went by too quickly, but we made plans to meet at Bill's family's cottage in Ontario in mid-August, making it easier to say goodbye.

Next in our travels, we spent a couple of weeks at two different campgrounds on Lake George. The campgrounds were fine, but in a couple of the nearby towns, we were surprised to find so many unaccommodating people. ("Service rendered grudgingly, if at all.") I mean, New York CITY people are downright GUSHY by contrast.

Have you ever read one of those Alfred Hitchcock or Rod Serling stories where Our Hero is traveling through the eerie backroads of The Deep South on a foggy night? Suddenly he is stopped by the local sheriff or equivalent—someone named Big Bubba Scuzball, who has squinty eyes, bad breath, and a pot belly. "Wheah you goin' in such a hurry?" snarls Scuzzy. "You wuz goin' 16 mph in a 15-mph zone. Didn' chu see the sign we had hid behind thet rock ovah theah?" Whereupon Our Hero's car is impounded and he's thrown to the alligators, never to be heard of again.

I am here to tell my own story about the backroads of The North. It begins in Warrensburg when Howard and I try to pick up our mail, which is sent by our mail-service to General Delivery wherever we go.

Usually getting our mail is nothing to write home about, as the saying goes. We arrive at the post office; my husband shows his ID; the postal employee looks at the little picture on the driver's license, occasionally checks the "Wanted" posters on the wall to see if there's a match, then locates our mail. A few friendly exchanges, and we're on our way.

Not this time. Right off the bat, the Person-Behind-The-Counter (PBTC) (mis)informs us that there's a ten-day limit on collecting General Delivery mail. According to her, after that people must rent a post office box, "*because we are a 'first-class' post office*" (her words).

What exactly was it that was "first-class"? Had the United States Postal Service suddenly developed a caste system, whereby post offices were rated by somebody like Duncan Hines—shiny stars for "First Class," mud-colored for "Low Class"?

Or did it serve only "first-class people"? Now this thought hurt: Had our PBTC decided we didn't qualify? Quelle horreur! What had gone wrong? We usually dress presentably; we'd worn our shoes that day, even our shirts.

Now we don't know *everything* about our postal system, but we think the rules are pretty universal. So a few days later we consulted the Postmaster Himself, who seemed as mystified as we about PBTC's remarks.

We never saw her again, leading us to believe she was never a bona fide postal employee at all, but an extra-terrestrial undergoing a bad-hair day who just happened to wander behind the counter at the very moment we arrived.

Must confess, we ran into one tiny facility in a tiny town that might have qualified for the muddy star. We drove up and down all six blocks of Main Street several times, looking in vain for the post office. It turned out to be housed inside a dingy "General Store," where you could also buy fishing licenses, booze, dusty cans of soda pop, worms, and other necessities of life. The postmaster/storekeeper more-or-less matched the decor, but at least he was nice.

I digress. Back to Warrensburg and our next stop, the local drug store to get a prescription refilled. No go. The minute I say the magic word "refill," the pharmacist interrupts to say that my physician will have to call it in *personally*. Everywhere else, the calls have been made pharmacy to pharmacy. So I call Dr. Carter, talk to Janice, the receptionist, who says she's surprised the *pharmacy* didn't call them, since pharmacies are usually happy to get the busine$$. Tell you what, say I, why don't you *mail* me the prescription. *Not* to Warrensburg—the extra-terrestrial might be counting my mail. Send it to Lake George, five miles away, and I'll find a pharmacy that's more customer-oriented.

Next chapter. We pick up the prescription from Lake George General Delivery without interrogation. Right next door is a building with a big sign that says "Rexall." Rexall! Rexall Drug Store! How convenient, you say. After wandering around among the T-shirts, cosmetics, and souvenirs for a while, I finally ask the person in the photo department where the pharmacy is.

"We don't *have* a pharmacy," he tells me grumpily.

Heavens! Silly me! Since no other information seems to be forthcoming, I venture to ask another foolish question, "Can you tell me where there *is* a pharmacy?" Across the street and down a block.

There it is: P-H-A-R-M-A-C-Y! Oooops, strike-out again. They don't have my prescription in stock. Again, no offer of alternatives. ("Could you come back tomorrow?" Or "There's a Walgreens nearby . . . .") So again I ask my foolish question. I'm told I might try in Glens Falls—another five miles away.

At last, in Glens Falls, our faith in human neighborliness is restored. The pharmacist doesn't have what I need, but he can get it by tomorrow, if I don't mind returning. Then, on the way out, we ask one of the clerks if he'd happen to know where the Triple-A office is. "No, but I'll find out," says he, as if he's actually glad to help people!

Oh well, all this gives us something to laugh about later.

At one of the Lake George campgrounds, most of our fellow campers were from Québec. When we pulled in with our New Mexico plates attached to our western-made fifth-wheel, we became an instant curiosity. Within minutes our neighbors Jacques and Francine came over to chat with us. Not long after, they and two other couples invited us to join them around their campfire.

They were all very friendly and encouraged us to stop in Québec before traveling on to Ontario. Seems our route often takes shape as we get suggestions from people we meet along the way.

The problems between the French-Canadians and the English-Canadians are very complex, and we don't begin to understand it all. But one of the sad things, we've heard more than once, is that many French feel themselves in a no-win situation. Even if they speak English, they are put down for speaking it with an accent.

Many Québec Canadians (Québécois) like the USA and feel they are treated much better by the Americans than by their fellow English-speaking countrymen. We were amused—and somewhat touched—by Jacques's description of our country: "Americans all fly their flags—every house has a flag—and they all like each other and are so friendly." Well, why not? And after all, who can argue with someone else's personal experiences?

ST. ANICET, QUÉBEC—July 23-29, 1992

Wouldn't you know, as we were driving here from New York, we missed the Canadian border and wound up on the Mohawk Reservation. Howard pulled into a service station and got out of the truck, map in hand. The owner—a rotund Native with wire-rim glasses and a wide smile—came outside laughing, put his arm around Howard's shoulder, and asked, "How lost are you?"

SO we made our U-turn and went back to "the" traffic light at Ft. Covington and turned north. (This brings a possible story title to mind: *Numerous U-Turns We Have Made.*)

We later ran into other people who'd missed the turn, mainly because the turn isn't marked the way you'd expect it—like with a big sign (or ANY kind of sign!) saying "CANADA →." There *was* a VERY SMALL hand-lettered sign saying "Customs Inspection" with an arrow slanting toward a tree, but somehow it didn't catch our eye.

We do like our campground here, despite the inadequate electrical system. We share a 15-amp hookup with another RV; so if one of us turns on the toaster, and the other the coffeepot, our common breaker trips. Of course, this is a handy way to meet one's neighbors, and ours turned out to be a congenial couple from Florida. We decided it was easier to take turns than to explain anything to the owner, who didn't seem to understand either our "foreign" language or our need for a little more juice.

We're enjoying Canadian television—we get French stations from Montreal and English channels from Ottawa—very little US news. (Now we know why Jacques's perceptions were uncolored by negative happenings.) We've seen some *Wonder Years* reruns with French dubbed in, and *Les Tortoises Ninja*.

The weather is given in Celsius. The high for the summer (so far) is 27°! Well, even translated to 80°, that's pretty mild for summer. We haven't seen 90° since we left Zapata. Not that we're complaining—it just seems strange for June and July.

All the campground rules are posted on a big board. #7 says "Ne pas lancer de roches sur la pelouse." Luckily, I remember a little of my high-school French, or Howard might have gone around lancing cockroaches on the peloozy.

Howard says speaking French would be made easier by stapling down the corners of one's mouth. The next-best remedy for good communication is to talk loudly in broken English. Nous allons, mes enfants.

The cutest little girls, about four or five years old, are staying a couple of doors down. One day when Howard was puttering around outside, they stopped on their way to the playground to ask him, "Do you steal people?"

"Only bad people," he told them. "Are you bad?"

"No," they said, "we mean, do you steal *kids*?"

So he assured them he didn't. I had to laugh—I'm pretty sure this method of checking out potential kidnappers is not what their folks had in mind!

WELLESLEY ISLAND, NEW YORK
July 30 through August 5, 1992

Thursday we arrived at "The 1000 Islands." We found an information sign that said the 1000 Islands used to be the "playground of the fabulously wealthy," but now it is enjoyed by people from all walks of life. "Thank goodness!" say we of the fabulously mediocre income.

Friday was rainy and cold, and, despite Park Rule #11, which reads

"ELECTRIC HEATERS ARE STRICTLY FORBIDDEN"

we turned on our small heater briefly to ward off frostbite. The list of rules also reads,

"ALL RULES WILL BE STRICTLY ENFORCED"

so we had to hope the electric-heater patrol wasn't out making its rounds.

Rule #16 reads, "Thoroughly enjoy your visit!" We wondered if there was an enjoyment patrol to enforce this one.

CRYSTAL BEACH RESORT—MADOC, ONTARIO
August 6-11, 1992

I guess retirement isn't for everyone. At ages 86 and 84, my folks are still working! They've signed with an acting agency and are frequently called for small parts in TV movies or to make commercials. When we picked up mail from home, we learned my mom had given my dad a sail-plane ride for his birthday. I suppose next year he'll want to try bungee jumping.

We also heard that our Behm grandkids are in a school district that's implementing the year-round system, so their classes have already started. Brendan loves school; Ben doesn't. Alas, the air conditioning in Ben's building isn't working (and it's hot in Albuquerque this time of year). Mary's a little disgruntled. She says it's hard enough just to get Ben to *go* to school, even at its best. I wonder if he's still seated next to the little girl with all the allergies.

As for us, we still enjoy puttering around. Madoc is a pretty little town—small and untouristy. We haven't found a T-shirt shop yet! We got here Thursday and parked by beautiful Moira Lake. Howard bought his fishing license and set up our little boat. He enjoys fishing, regardless of whether or not the fish enjoy biting.

The weather people have predicted a storm—the picture on the TV map showed beautiful weather all over the USA and Canada except for a big dark cloud over this part of Ontario. The Canadians are disappointed that this summer hasn't been sunnier, and we can sympathize, especially since their summers are so short. But we couldn't work up much sympathy when we heard someone from *Florida* complaining.

LAKE OF BAYS, ONTARIO
August 17-25, 1992

We spent a pleasant week with Louise and Bill at Bill's family's cottage in Lake of Bays. After greeting us with heavy rain, the weather cleared, and we took advantage of the balmy days to hike and "leaf-peek." Louise and I also enjoyed browsing the library in nearby Baysville and a used-book store in Bracebridge, another neighboring town.

One chilly evening we sat around the fireplace while Louise read aloud an old favorite: Kipling's *The Cat That Walked By Himself.*

The mornings were quite brisk (translate, freezing cold), but Bill plunged into the lake every morning for an invigorating swim, while Louise and I watched from the warmth of our cozy cabin, wrapped in comforters. Howard was brave enough to join Bill one morning, but quickly returned, claiming he was one degree short of having hypothermia.

Another evening we had dinner at the family farm near Barrie with Bill's cousins. We knew that butter tarts were a Canadian specialty, but Susan's were the most mouth-watering we found.

For me, the most magical experience of all was my first encounter with loons. I was completely transfixed by their haunting cries.

SUDBURY, ONTARIO—August 26, 1992

After spending a few delightful weeks in Canada without terrifying anyone with our driving habits, we headed home. Suddenly we found ourselves in downtown Sudbury at rush hour, having (typically) missed a turn-off somewhere along the way. It looked as if another U-turn was in store. (U-turns made while maneuvering a 30-foot trailer are even more fun than your run-of-the-mill variety.)

But we were in for a pleasant surprise. At the traffic light, I rolled down my window and asked the sweet young thing in the sports car next to us how to find our missing highway.

"Follow me," she said. When the light changed, she zipped in front of us and led us through a labyrinth of streets till we arrived at the proper destination. With a warm smile and a wave of her hand, she indicated we'd arrived, then made her own U-turn to go back to wherever she'd been headed before going out of her way to help strangers.

SAULT STE. MARIE, MICHIGAN
August 27-30, 1992

You'll be relieved to know that we didn't embarrass ourselves by mispronouncing Sault Ste. Marie. Everyone knows, of course, that "Sault" rhymes with "Sioux," as in the song, *Sioux City Sault,* or that Johnny Cash favorite, *A Boy Named Sault.*

One afternoon we rode the ferry from St. Ignace to Mackinac Island. No automobiles are allowed on the island, which surely makes it nice for the overabundance of pedestrian traffic. You would love the main drag—fudge shops everywhere! Now here are some folks with their priorities in order.

Instead of tour buses or trolleys to accommodate sightseers, the town provides horse-drawn carriages, the fragrance doing battle with the fudge. So we preferred to walk, and once we made our way to the side streets, we found the sights more interesting and the horses (and pedestrians) less numerous. The "summer cottages" there are spectacular—talk about fabulous wealth—and it's fun to wander by and gawk.

We also visited the "Soo Locks" (why on earth, you're asking, would somebody want to spell Sault "s-o-o"?) and watched some large ships navigate the St. Marys River into Canada.

ALONG THE WAY—September 1992

Where to next? Howard wanted to go to Branson, Missouri— "The New Nashville." I had just read an article about Branson's legendary traffic problems. It's estimated that 10,000 vehicles a day pass through a town whose normal population is about 3,000. Let's just say I didn't relish the idea of going there; but we decided the pluses outweighed the minuses.

On the way, we stopped in Springfield (Missouri) for a couple of days to visit my cousin Ann and to explore Bass Pro—"the *world's* largest sporting-goods store." We hadn't realized this was such a major attraction, almost rivaling Branson's musical shows. Howard went because he wanted to get a new bass rod, but the aisles were filled with people who'd evidently come to take pictures of themselves. Wish I could get residuals for all the home movies I must be in.

Our RV park was nice and quiet during the day. But at night we were treated to the strangest noise. I thought it was made by a flying-saucer manufacturing company, as it clamped (slammed/ clanged) the top half onto the bottom half of the spaceship, the way babies bang pots and pans' lids together, only much louder of course, because of the immense size. (I'm here to tell you if those UFO people want to keep their activities secret, they'd better find a quieter way to go about it.) Howard thought the sound was made by railroad cars coupling, but his version sounded pretty far-fetched to me.

Some really unusual people pulled into the park not long after we got there. It wasn't that these folks weren't pleasant—you'd be hard put to find nicer people. But compared to theirs, our lifestyle is rigidly structured.

Eldon was in his mid-sixties; Tina, his wife, thirty-something; their son, five. We never found out the little boy's name—he insisted it was "Monster Man." Eldon had sold their home in Colorado, bought a very short trailer he didn't know how to tow, packed his family and all their belongings into it, and was on his way to Branson to become a famous songwriter.

They'd been staying in KOA campgrounds along the way, until they ran into someone in town who told them there were less expensive places and brought them to our campground to look it over. Eldon wanted to know how we'd found out about this neat park, and we told him it was listed in the *Trailer Life Directory*, which he'd never heard of (which to us is the "bible" of RVers, and as necessary as a roadmap).

Next, Eldon decided he liked *our* spot and wanted to park there, but Howard explained that we were already *there*, so to speak. But we'd be leaving in a couple of days and he could have our site then. In the meantime, Eldon thought he might like to park right beside us—like a couple of inches away. Since he was so inexperienced at handling his trailer, his efforts to back in were a tad hair-raising. Fortunately the manager came to the rescue, telling Eldon that the space was already reserved. I don't know where they went next; we didn't see them anymore. (Maybe they found out about the flying saucer factory.)

Even though it was funny on the surface (and the whole thing did seem sort of surreal), there was something a little sad too. Tina seemed rather lonely underneath her brave smile, so I hope they find a place where they can settle in and she can make friends. And we also can't help hoping that, although we chuckled over Eldon's life in the twilight zone, he realizes his dream and has the last laugh after all.

On to Branson. The traffic was what we expected, but drivers unexpectedly courteous. We were parked about three miles east of town, well away from the throngs. We saw some of our favorite performers—Loretta Lynn, Roy Clark, and Don Williams—and thought their shows were great.

Best of all, we stumbled upon a wonderful barbecue place called Odie's in nearby Forsyth. Mark this on your game-plan if you ever go to Branson. Skip Boxcar Willie if you must, but don't miss Odie's!

After leaving Branson, we traveled through Arkansas and the scenic Ozarks on our way *home*. Now that we've decided to change our "official" residence to Texas, the odd thing is that I, the Texas native, feel reluctant to give up New Mexico residency, while Howard, the Chicago native, is eager to become a Texan! In any event, we're both looking forward to returning to Zapata.

ZAPATA, TEXAS
October 16 through December 31, 1992

October 24, 1992

Here we are, back in mañana-land. Not too many changes—the plaque in the town square still reads, "ELCOME TO ZAPATA," and the driver's license tests are still done at the Lions Club on Wednesdays, if someone shows up to give them. And there's still just one traffic light.

It's been fun to be among the first to arrive—to find some friends already here, and to greet others as they come in. Having said this, we think we might have been wise to wait another week. All summer long we found ourselves staying wherever the weather was breaking record lows. (In other words, we froze to death.) Didn't turn on our air conditioner from the end of March till the middle of September, and nearly wore out our sweatshirts.

Then when we finally got back here, the middle of October, the weatherman said we were breaking record *highs*. I'm here to say, HOT AND MUGGY. But we have a nice site—the one we had our first time here—and get a pleasant lake breeze.

We've enjoyed our walks, as well as "just settin' still" and watching the birds and the changing colors of the lake. It's too early for the pelicans, but we've seen several egrets, some exotic-looking green jays, and the same cocky squawky grackles. The purple sage needs rain before it blooms, but the bougainvillea is in full splendor.

I went to Mass last Sunday, and nothing has changed there either. The parishioners seem to me like the nice sort of people you'd find in any congregation, but Father is always giving them hell about something.

This week he was berating people who "drop their children off for Mass and then drive away in their Cadillacs," and he wasn't going to let them get away with it, and they could just go to the Baptist Church next week or whatever. (I might have left something out—my mind wandered a little during this discourse.)

Of course, the people he was mad at weren't there to hear his lecture, and those of us who hadn't dropped anyone off from our Cadillacs got to be the captive audience.

I happened to see Father in the grocery store not long after that, laughing and chatting with a couple of parishioners, his eyes twinkling. Catching this glimpse of him helped me get a different perspective.

November 20, 1992

My folks flew from Phoenix to New York for Louise and Bill's wedding the middle of October. Unfortunately the trip was too strenuous for them. My dad developed a fever and wound up in the hospital the day before the wedding. Louise and Bill had originally planned to be married at home, with just a few friends and family members present; instead, everyone met at the hospital, and the service was performed in the chapel there so Pop could attend.

He was fairly weak, and somewhat fuzzy from the medication, so Louise wasn't sure how much he remembered. But the next day when she asked him about it, his eyes lit up. "Oh, yes," he answered. "It was a *beautiful* wedding!" She couldn't have asked for a better gift.

A few days later, Pop underwent prostate surgery, then seemed to go back and forth healthwise. Louise was beginning to get alarmed, so I flew up to New York to be with them. Fortunately, he began a steady upward trend not long after I got there. He spent another week in the hospital, then convalesced at "home" (Louise and Bill's) the following week.

It was certainly a relief to get him home. I used to think a hospital was a good place to be if you were sick, but I'm beginning to wonder. The nurses were great, but there just weren't enough of them, and the hospital itself seemed a little bizarre. It wasn't very large, but it took me a few days to find my way around—I kept winding up in the psychiatric wing. (Is there a message here?)

I finally got the hang of the floor plan, however. All I had to do was follow the sign that said, "2 South is now 4 North," and go through the door marked "Positively No Admittance," and look for the wing with pictures of Bambi on the walls. (Yep, Pop was on the maternity floor.)

But the floor plan was the least of our worries. The main reason for Pop's extra days in the hospital was to regain his strength, and the doctor left orders for a physical therapist to come in. Ooooops, the PT didn't work on weekends. Monday came. Ooooops, the PT forgot. So Mom, Louise, and I began taking Pop through our own version of exercises in the meantime.

Then one day a lung specialist visited Pop. Ooooops, wrong patient. Pop was feeling better by then, and very indignant. He said he was glad they didn't just waltz in and lop something off.

His last morning there, some woman (lab technician? candy striper? postal employee?) came in his room and said she was there for his blood test. He said he shouldn't need one since he was being discharged that morning. She said he had to have it anyway "in preparation for the transfusion."

"What transfusion?" he asked.

So she shuffled through her paperwork. Ooooops, wrong patient. (I can't imagine having a baby in this hospital—they'd probably stick it in the geriatrics ward where it would never be heard of again.)

Anyway, we finally got Pop back home with his own blood, lungs, and other bodily parts intact. He continued to improve, and I returned to Zapata last week. The folks went back to Phoenix the next day. My daughters/their granddaughters Valerie and Linda will be helping with meals and such.

I'm glad I went up to New York, but am also glad to be in Zapata again where the pace is slower. I read in our weekly paper that a lot happened while I was gone. The ballot boxes got impounded. And the front-page story of the week was about someone getting bitten by his neighbor's dog.

But I don't want you to think this place is *too* small town. While looking up something in the yellow pages, I happened to spot a heading for "Nudist Organizations" with a subheading that read "See *Clubs*." So I looked under "Clubs" and found only *one*: "Club Los Amigos." On that same page, I saw "Clubs— Automobile" with the same subheading: "See *Clubs*." So I can only assume that Zapata boasts a nudist automobile club called "Club Los Amigos." A little too racy for me, if you'll pardon the pun.

Once again, after settling in, we're flying away—this time to Phoenix for Thanksgiving. This trip should be fun. Pop is feeling much better, and I think his recovery is a timely reminder of all we have to be thankful for.

*   *   *

(Ne pas lancer de roches sur la pelouse: Don't throw rocks on the lawn.)

1993

ZAPATA, TEXAS
January 1 through March 17, 1993

January 12, 1993

It's a cold bleak day here, a good day for staying indoors, brewing hot spiced tea, and cranking up the ol' computer . . . .

Howard and I began taking conversational Spanish courses at the library with Adán Gutierrez. Howard's in a beginning class, and already starting to get the pronunciation down quite well. I'm in an intermediate class, trying not to sound like a hick in two languages.

I just flew back from a wonderful visit in Albuquerque, where I met our newest granddaughter, Aubrey Shannon Behm. I'd forgotten what it was like to suddenly notice that it was 1:00 or 2:00 in the afternoon and wonder if I'd remembered to brush my teeth. I marvel at all the things Mary can do one-handed; yet there were times when, even with four, six, or eight hands pitching in, we still arrived at mid-day with unbrushed teeth.

Also had fun playing cards with Ben and Brendan. Ben's reached the age where he can laugh and be a good sport when Grandma whips the socks off him. Brendan has his own version of the rules, otherwise he still has a happy disposition.

On my return flight, I sat next to a little girl from Santa Fe. She was about nine years old, and not a happy camper. After we'd been in the air about four minutes, she said she thought she was going to throw up. This didn't seem to faze her mother, so I guess it was just a routine whine. After she'd knocked over her Coca Cola and stomped off to the restroom a few times, she seemed to forget about throwing up.

I suppose it's pretty boring to be nine years old and flying all the way to Philadelphia, so after a while we got to chatting, and I found her to be kind of cute. I really laughed when we landed at the Dallas airport. Looking out the window at the runway and other nondescript scenery, she announced, "This doesn't look like Texas. Where are all the cows?" Once inside the airport, she asked, "Where are all the cowboys?"

From Dallas to Laredo, the plane was cold, so I'd bundled up accordingly. When we arrived in Laredo, it was 75°! I looked like the abominable snowman, and felt equally out of place. We had another lovely day Saturday before this cold front set in.

February 20-24, 1993

Our daughter Valerie flew into Corpus Christi, where we met her plane. Then we crossed Laguna Madre Bay to the Padre Island National Seashore, one of our favorite places to take beach walks. Back in Zapata, Valerie and Howard caught a slew of catfish one afternoon, and we continued relaxing throughout her visit. She decided the slow pace wouldn't suit her forever, but it was exactly what she needed at the time.

March 15, 1993

It's that time of year when folks head for cooler climates. I find it easier to tell friends goodbye knowing we'll meet here again next fall.

Our daughter Sharon says that where she's working this winter (Sanibel Island, Florida), people live in one of two places: "here" and "North." I think that's true of Zapata too. Zapata is "here." Everywhere else is "North." Our "northern" destination is Phoenix.

A few weeks ago my dad drove to the neighborhood bank and fell in the parking lot, apparently while getting out of his car. We'll never know exactly what happened, but his watch and wallet weren't taken, so at least we know he wasn't a victim of robbery.

Pop was found unconscious by someone who called 911. Whoever found him didn't stay with him, and it bothered me a lot to think of him lying there alone and helpless. The paramedics came and took him to the hospital, where he was diagnosed with a concussion. Once they identified him, they called my mother. My sister and I plan to take turns staying with the folks during Pop's convalescence.

PHOENIX, ARIZONA
April 1 through May 4, 1993

My dad has not been doing well since his accident. The pain has subsided, but he has deteriorated both physically and mentally. Worst of all is his depression. He had been so upbeat following his illness in New York, confident that he was on the road to recovery. Now he seems to feel hopeless.

Becky, one of the wonderful health-care nurses, recommended someone she knows to live in with the folks. Even though it's touchy to suggest to Mom that *she* needs help too, we're feeling optimistic about the new arrangements.

ALBUQUERQUE, NEW MEXICO
May 6 through June 8, 1993

Our time in Arizona and in Albuquerque went by quickly. We had fun with family and friends, but did some un-fun things too. Up till now, whenever we'd peer into our too-large cinderblock storage room, we'd say, "ooooh, aaaaah," slam the door shut, and hope not to look inside again for another year or two. We finally forced ourselves to condense our junk to fit another storage room about one-third the size. This isn't nearly so rewarding as gardening.

One afternoon we went to the zoo with our daughter Mary and our grandkids. We had a delightful time viewing the new baby animals. The baby elephant (Rosie) was especially cute (if that's the appropriate word for a wrinkly, hairy, 200-pound. infant). The mama ushered Rosie close to the fence so everyone could get a good look. Some of the animals like to hide, but these seemed to enjoy the attention.

GRAND TETONS NATIONAL PARK
June 13-19, 1993

From Albuquerque we meandered up toward the Grand Tetons, where Sharon is working this summer, for our family mini-reunion. We had a wooded site at Colter Bay RV Park, where we could see the majestic Tetons across the lake.

The kids were great. They seemed to get along well (with only minor skirmishes), and—between horseback-riding, aerial-tram-riding, and discovering the Alpine slide—certainly never had time to get bored. We adults were great too, and had fun touring "The Mangy Moose" (a bar and non-mangy gift shop) and the Chocolate Factory.

We also stopped by to see the Mural Room, where Sharon works. On one side of the restaurant are floor-to-ceiling windows, all with a magnificent view of the Tetons. But not everyone appreciates the view. One evening Sharon had a customer who asked her to "do something about the sun." Since adjusting the blinds didn't help, and since adjusting the sun was a little out of Sharon's bailiwick, the best she could offer was for the lady to change tables. But the lady preferred to gripe.

From then on, we kidded Sharon about being in charge of Nature. Mary overheard a woman (probably the same one) complaining to the ranger during our one-and-only rainy day, "When does the weather ever get pleasant around here?" she asked.

The ranger told her, "In April." Maybe he was hoping she'd go away and not come back till then. Mary thought he should have told the woman to ask *Sharon* what she intended to do about the weather.

THAYNE, WYOMING—June 20-26, 1993

After everyone else went home, Howard and I drove down to Thayne. For some reason, the sites in this campground are arranged in groups of four RVs squished together, each squished-up group separated by a skinny strip of grass. Some sites are packed, some virtually empty. Who gets parked where depends on the person sitting at the check-in gate, and what kind of mood he's in, I guess.

From our back windows we have a very sharp close-up view of the windshield wipers of a monster Winnebago. Luckily, there is no one *next* to us for several spaces, and from our dining- and living-room windows we can see mountains covered with evergreens, and beyond these, even higher, snow-capped mountains. So we've enjoyed our other views, especially at mealtime.

We'd made plans to meet with Sharon again in Jackson Hole, so didn't have to go cold turkey on goodbyes. We met on the third day of summer (June 23), and got snowed upon! So it felt good to be sitting inside Sweetwater's, a cozy restaurant that specializes in Greek cooking. After warming ourselves with lots of hot tea and enjoying a delicious meal, we walked over to Thomas Mangelsen's gallery, where we were entranced by all his wildlife photography, especially the photos of polar bears.

The sun doesn't know when to quit up here. Sunset starts about 9:30, and it isn't dark till about 10:00. We never know when it's mealtime, so we've solved that problem by eating constantly.

ROCK CREEK, MONTANA—July 1-5, 1993

Let me tell you all about that big Montana sky. We've seen very little of it. Mostly it's been covered by big black clouds. The high (temperature) has been in the 60s, and was only 55° Tuesday. Yes, it IS July.

One afternoon Howard and I went to a restaurant in Missoula called McKays on the River. Not only was the food good, but the owner had an abundance of memorabilia on display. What I found most fascinating was the framed sheet music that lined the walls in every room. Much of the music dated back from World War I, with titles such as *I Didn't Raise My Boy to be a Soldier*, and *I'll Come Back to You When It's All Over*. The illustrations were also quite sentimental, some of young soldiers saying goodbye to their mothers. (All the mothers looked to be 110 years old.)

A pileated woodpecker surprised us one evening by appearing right outside our door. We've read that this species of woodpecker makes itself scarce whenever people are around, but this one seemed oblivious to our presence as it hammered away at a log.

LEWIS-CLARK RESORT, KAMIAH, IDAHO
July 14-20, 1993

Last Wednesday we traveled from Lolo, Montana, into Kamiah, Idaho, via Highway 12, the "Wild-and-Scenic River Corridor." It was certainly scenic, surrounded by mountains and an abundance of evergreens and flowers, with the river—sometimes rapid, sometimes smooth—paralleling the road. Happy to say, "wild" described the flowers, plus a few deer, and not the highway itself.

We noticed the same sign we'd seen in Idaho two years ago: "Watch for Rock." Evidently they haven't found it yet.

Yesterday was sunny and warm for the first time in weeks, and I went outdoors without a coat! Today (July 19) is sunny/cloudy; the weatherman from Spokane (the closest TV news—150 miles away) said we'd be having "all twelve hours of summer" today, before the thunderstorms return. Willard Scott's map showed normal, below normal, and above normal temps for the rest of the country, but our little corner was labeled something like "super below normal." Keep reminding us we came up north to get cool . . . .

One Christmas, my mom gave us some "Map of the USA" placemats. We use them not just as table covers, but also as conversation pieces. They're there to remind us of where we've been or where we'd like to go, and we consult our place mats at every meal, which is not to say we *plan* anything that often, but it's fun looking.

Something we discovered in our belated study of geography is that the *southern* border of Montana is on the same parallel as the *northern*most border of New York. (And we have a "placemap" to prove it.) Just hadn't realized New York was so close to the Mason-Dixon line, or that Toronto, Ontario, is farther south than Missoula, Montana.

This reminded us of another discovery we'd made last fall while in New York near the Canadian border. There we saw a restaurant advertising "south-of-the-border" cuisine. At first we thought it meant Mexican food, but it finally dawned on us that from Canada, "south" is the US. Exactly what kind of cuisine they served, we didn't investigate—Hamburger Helper, maybe? (The stuff my kids grew up on?)

And whoever thinks of Mexico as "west of the border"? But that's where it is in relation to Zapata. In fact, "north of the border" can describe Mexico from Zapata as well.

Well, the sun came out, and we have to—hurry-quick—enjoy one of our allotted twelve hours of summer . . . .

COEUR D'ALENE, IDAHO—July 21-27, 1993

Surprise, surprise! We had two partly sunny days in a row! The weather people say the temperature has been 14° lower than normal, and 80° has yet to be seen. But at least it warmed up to 76°, which brought droves of people outdoors.

Sunday we took a hike around Tubbs Hill, a 120-acre natural park in the middle of town. The three-mile trail encircling the park is well-maintained, the climb fairly easy to negotiate. Along the first stretch of the trail, we could look down through evergreens to Lake Coeur d'Alene below. Even after we'd curved away from the lake, we continued to enjoy the beauty of the wooded surroundings.

We inadvertently took a "short-cut" near the end of our hike. It was short, all right, and a lot more vertical than these old knees are used to. But the scenery was worth it, and I got to collect lots of *weeds*. Weeds, you say!

Yes, my latest treasure is a grocery sack full of teasel weeds, which I'll use with the grandchildren to make little "critters." If I *must* collect things, Howard can be glad I don't collect boulders the way Lucille Ball did when she and Desi took off in their *Long Long Trailer.*

But parting is never easy—whether it's giving up all these sea-shells (from so many beaches, I've lost track of which is which), or excess pine cones, or sand-dollars, or Dungeness crab shells. I finally gave most of my rocks to our grandson Brendan.

After misspelling and mispronouncing names all across the USA, I always feel an affinity for others facing the same dilemma. At the bottom of Tubbs Hill, we saw some people examining a license plate from New Mexico—Sandoval County, to be exact. They pronounced it to rhyme with "oval." So it sounded like, "San Doval" (some obscure Spanish saint, no doubt).

CROSSING THE BORDER—August 3, 1993

From Coeur d'Alene we went to an RV park in the woods in Washington, to enjoy the *warm sun* and scenery. Here it was the first of August, and summer had finally arrived! From there we came into Canada.

Don't know why, but for some reason I seem to get homesick whenever we cross into Canada. Suddenly we're in the land of Celsius, kilometers, and funny money; and all these worrisome questions come to mind: Will they search our rig? (Yep.) Will they slash open my teddy bear looking for smuggled diamonds? (Nope.) How fast can we drive going 100 km/h? How many dollars in a dollar? What's the weather like when I hear they're expecting a "scorching" 30°? Should I add, or maybe subtract, 32° before, or maybe after, I either multiply or divide 5/9—or is it 9/5—to the Celsius number?

Usually once we get further down the road (and my teddy bear has recovered from the trauma), things begin to look up. This time things seemed to continue downward. We were headed for Waterton Lakes, the Canadian part of the Waterton-Glacier International Peace Park. (The US section of the park, the larger section, is better known in our country as Glacier National Park.) We had planned to stop about halfway along the way. The only

RV park we found (following—you guessed it—one of our infamous U-turns) was somewhat gloomy and run-down, but we figured for one night it didn't matter.

No one was in the office, but there was a sign telling people to park anywhere they liked and pay up later. When the manager finally did arrive, she wasn't happy with the space we'd chosen. I think she was just naturally disagreeable; another group felt so unwelcome they decided to leave. So much for the red-carpet treatment.

WATERTON, ALBERTA, CANADA
August 4-6, 1993

The next day we felt bright and optimistic as we headed for Waterton. Our luck with RV parks shifted even further down the scale. The current one is spectacularly ugly. Bet you never expected me to say *that*! It looked, at first glance, like a salvage yard, with abandoned rusty cars lined up against a barbed wire fence overgrown with weeds. On closer inspection, it still looked seedy AND it turned out to be very expensive. Not having "Plan B" in mind, we went ahead and checked in, but decided to stay only a few nights instead of the week we'd originally intended.

The good news is that we spent most of our time at Waterton Lakes anyway, which we thoroughly enjoyed. The weather was cooperative, and the hiking trails well-planned. The village of Waterton was charming, although it seemed odd to see deer and bighorn sheep (with little horns) wandering amiably around town. The townspeople seemed pretty blasé, but the rest of us had our cameras out.

Sometimes I wish cameras could capture fragrances. At Red Rock, the mingled scent of wild roses, sweet yellow clover, and white clover was heavenly. However, when the sheep showed up, we had second thoughts about the odor-indicator.

We ran into some people who were a little distraught because all the national park campgrounds were filled, and they didn't know where to stay. Although their camper was pretty dilapidated (I think the whole thing was held together with duct tape and hope), when I suggested they might stay at *our* RV park, the mother looked horrified and said, "Oh, we couldn't stay *there*—that one's *Terrible*!" A place too dismal even for the Kallikaks.

It's interesting to hear US news from a Canadian perspective; I get the impression they consider us completely barbaric. Not that Canada is without crime, but apparently the level of violence is greater in the States. Canadians seem genuinely mystified by the raging debate over the inalienable right of every man, woman, and child in America to own assault weapons.

This reminds me—our daughter Linda said that Arizona was considering legislation that would allow children to carry weapons "with parental consent." Linda said she could see herself writing a note to Adrienne's first-grade teacher:

"Dear Mrs. Black, it's OK with me if Adrienne brings her M16 to school."

ST. MARY, MONTANA—August 13, 1993

After leaving Waterton, we came to St. Mary, Montana, and Glacier National Park, where we continued hiking and marveling. I had long ago given up hope of ever seeing any bears. We've hiked in the Smokies, Yellowstone, the Grand Tetons, and have seen lots of flora and fauna, but nary a bear. (Although Howard surprised, or was surprised by, black bears on a couple of occasions in New Mexico.) I don't count the one bear that was so far away that, even with binoculars, you could have told me it was a ground squirrel, and I wouldn't have known the difference.

I especially didn't expect to see any bears while we hiked the designated "Easy Trail" around Swiftcurrent Lake, in mid-afternoon, with lots of tourists nearby. So we were quite surprised to turn a corner and see a crowd looking across the highway at what someone said was a big grizzly. (Here we go again, I thought: another speck.) We walked closer and were looking for specks in the cliffs, when someone clued us in that the bear was just across the road—less than fifty yards away! Quite exciting to see a grizzly so close!

Bears have never been known to charge a large crowd here at Glacier, so we felt pretty safe—even safer to see the park ranger keeping an eye on things. This bear was simply strolling around, nonchalantly munching on weeds, and ignoring us spectators.

One thing about these parks that are well known for wildlife: Whenever a car stops, everyone else along the road stops to see whatever it is the first person saw. Soon there are lots of cars lined up, with folks getting out holding binoculars, cameras, etc., saying, "Where is it? What are we looking for?"

One day it was foggy and chilly, but we decided to take a short nature hike anyway. Couple of bonuses for picking a foggy, chilly day. First of all, it was very uncrowded; we didn't see *anyone* else on the path. Most of all, we saw things with "new eyes." The dew gave everything a new dimension. Even the spider webs, always fragile and lacy, looked radiant and pearly. Many of the flowers looked "sparkly," and some of the fuzzy ones almost like crystal.

And there was such a large colorful variety of wildflowers. I wish I could tell you all their names—something more distinctive than "little teeny white things," and "tall purple fluffy things." But, except for buttercups, dandelions, lupine, and Indian paintbrush, I'm pretty ignorant.

You see, I still haven't conquered the mysteries of my guidebook. Either I can't find pictures to match the flowers or, when I do, they often have such ugly names they don't stick in my memory. (Who on earth dreamed up "goatsbeard salsify" or "lousewort" or "hairy fleabane"?) And the scientific terminology means as much to me as advanced hieroglyphics.

Another hike took us along the "Highline Trail." It was fairly level but had been carved out of the side of a cliff and was very narrow in places, making me acrophobic. You could look down and see the highway where one misstep would send you hurtling.

Howard, of course, being the sure-footed Scout that he is, had no qualms. I followed the trail about a mile before wimping out, but Howard continued on. On the way back, I rounded a corner, looked up and saw a mountain goat peeking over a ledge just a few feet above me. To me this was as exciting as seeing the grizzly.

Other hikers had stopped to see him too, so he came out into full view to look us over. He had a comical look on his face, as if he were as curious about us as we were about him. Only difference, he didn't have his camera.

You'll be happy to know that while waiting for Howard, I checked out the Visitor Center and bought some wildflower books that not only had better photography, but also commentary I could understand. And some pretty names: candytuft, spring beauty, fairy primrose . . . . (Can't get away from lousewort, but that's the way it goes.)

While we enjoyed the international park on both sides of the border, we touched only the tip of the glacier, so to speak. I think we'd have to stay a whole summer (maybe longer) to see everything.

Someone pointed out that "Glacier National Park" might have been more aptly named "Glacier *Lakes* National Park." Not many glaciers are left (something we hadn't known before; I was expecting to see a lot). At least the melting glaciers have shaped some spectacular scenery.

*   *   *

Today is the 23rd of August, and only the second day this summer we've experienced hot weather. The high was 83°. It was nice to take off the parka.

The reason you don't see the name of the place where we are, is that I don't *know* where we are—somewhere in the twilight zone, I suspect. There was a town listed in our campground directory, a few miles south of the Idaho/Utah border, that we couldn't find on the map. However, we figured we would follow the directions in the directory; surely they hadn't simply invented this town and RV park. Well, I'm not sure what they invented, but I think it was a new way of determining north, south, east, and west, and a new highway-numbering system.

We were just about to make a U-turn when we spotted a sign pointing to the very RV park we were looking for. But it was not in the town where it was listed, in the direction we were supposed to take, or anywhere near the highway it was supposed to be on. But at least we are SOMEWHERE safe for the night, enjoying a beautiful sunset and lots of black-eyed Susans.

PHOENIX, ARIZONA
October 4, 1993

After spending time in Colorado and New Mexico, we arrived in Phoenix. I was glad to be here with my folks; at the same time, it was very difficult and sad to see Pop slowly slipping away. He's so thin and frail, and barely has the energy to speak above a whisper—not that he has much to say.

Seeing our daughters and granddaughters brightens our days. And today a "cooling trend" begins—so say the weather people. It's supposed to go down to 101°. (This gives you some idea.) By Friday it's supposed to be down to 90°—hope there isn't a run on snow shovels. They've been promising this cooler weather for two weeks. Guess they figure one of these days it'll be January, and their prediction will come true.

November 1993

Sad news: Pop died October 19. Since he'd been sick for so long, we knew it was the right time. Still, in some unexplainable way, it seemed quite a shock when the time actually came.

My mother handled her grief by denying it. She would forestall displays of emotion by saying things like, "It was really a blessing," or "It's all for the best," whenever people offered their condolences.

"We must let Marian know," she told me. Marian was a 91-year-old friend who lived in a nearby nursing home.

So we made our "duty visit" to tell Marian about Pop's death. She was sitting in her wheelchair with a multicolored afghan draped over her knees. Though on oxygen and physically ridden with a number of other ailments, she was still sharp mentally.

After giving Marian the news, Mom gave her standard "everything-is-fine" speech. Behind her round-rimmed glasses,

Marian's large brown eyes grew solemn and bewildered. At first she didn't respond; then she said very softly, "But how can the world go on turning without Malcolm in it?"

Her words went straight to my heart. This was what *I* felt, but hadn't known how to express.

Mom and I did share some lighter moments. Pop's wish was to be cremated, and the mortuary had given Mom a price list of the various containers for the ashes. The prices ranged from $70.00 for a plain cardboard box to $5000.00 for an urn that was quite ornate, velvet-lined, with gold inlay and other extravagant designs that I can't recall.

"Humph," Mom said. "For that price, you'd think they'd be air-conditioned."

Her remark sent us both into gales of hysterical laughter— probably a necessary release from the strain of the past few days.

One of the bright spots of October was seeing Linda receive her master's degree in education, after years of juggling family, teaching, and night classes. Watching her walk across that stage to get her diploma brought the same maternal thrill as watching her take her first baby steps.

ZAPATA, TEXAS
November 5 through December 31, 1993

I try to have my cake and eat it too by considering every day from Thanksgiving through Twelfth Night "the Christmas Season." Thus I was able to spend "the holidays" with all of our Phoenix/ Albuquerque family, and still be here with Howard on those special days.

Much as I enjoyed my visits, it was good to get home to Zapata again. The county put up Christmas lights in the plaza this year, and Howard had our palm tree all lit up, so everything looked quite festive. We celebrated Christmas Eve at the Methodist Church, then enjoyed mild weather and a potluck at our park on the 25th. How thankful we are to have good friends to share it with.

Maybe we appreciated it all the more because some of our friends didn't come back for one reason or another. In fact, when we first got here in November, we faced a number of disappointments. The park seemed a little drab, no rainfall, lake down, fish not biting—just a combination of things.

But we gradually got back in the swing of things—or maybe I should say the calm of things. And the slower pace is definitely soothing.

1994

ZAPATA, TEXAS
January 1 through April 12, 1994

January 1, 1994

Here's how we spent New Year's Eve: We parked ourselves in front of the TV, ate popcorn, and listened to the coyotes. All in all, a good way to start the year, I think. It's our hope that 1994—and the years to come—will find us all happy and healthy. Heck, why not wise and wealthy too?

We heard a message at church reminding us that the big umbrella called "family" includes *many* family units close to our hearts—often overlapping. We grow up in one family, maybe create another, maybe "inherit" another, adopt, extend, regroup; then watch a new generation continue the process. But "home" is always where we're centered.

One of the things we're attuned to right now is the pleasure of watching our children create their own homes. I think I was *first* aware of this when I went to Panama and discovered my daughter Mary had become a young woman in her own right, capable of smashing insects on her own. Seeing her wield that fly-swatter was quite impressive!

The weather here is like a ping-pong game, balmy one day, dreary the next. One pleasant day, I had a little misadventure resulting from my rapidly advancing Old-Timer's Disease. From the kitchen window, I saw Howard soaking up the sun while reading a book, and thought to myself, What a good idea! So I went outside to sit with him.

Soon we heard "trickle, trickle, trickle," and, lo and behold, the sink-water I'd forgotten to turn off was sloshing down the sides of the trailer and heading for the lake.

When I told Linda about this later, she said she'd done similar things. Not long ago she filled the tub for a bubble bath, turned the water off, but got distracted and never took her bath. She didn't discover it till some people came over to look at their house (which is up for sale) and found the tub filled with—by now bubbleless—bathwater.

I think we might need to circulate a family mental-health newsletter to reassure ourselves that either

a. we're all normal, or
b. we're all equally nutty.

By the way, Sharon decided to spend her WINTER in MICHIGAN, of all places. Why? you ask. Why? everybody asks. Her friends persuaded her to move there and go to Michigan State. They told her that Michigan has such a thing as "indoor heating." Anyway, she's happy, so we're happy.

Now for our latest venture. Adán became ill and was unable to continue teaching his popular Spanish classes at the library. So guess who was elected to teach a conversational class at our RV park? Would you believe, moi? I mean, ¿yo?

We started out with a small group (three people) which quickly grew to ten. Now we have a second group of ten. I'm excited about it! So far, it's proving to be fun, and I think I can stay ahead of the game for a while, at least till I get to the point that we can *ir al Jacal de Pizza* (go to the Pizza Hut) fluently.

Maybe next year I'll teach para-sailing.

April 8, 1994

Here we are, still in Zapata! As the weather warmed up, the fishing got better, so we aren't in any hurry to move on.

Up till now we've had very little rain, and the lake level is down. In fact the dry season has affected everything. We haven't seen as many birds this year, and the bluebonnets have been sparse. On the other hand, every spring surprises us with what *does* bloom. The honey mesquite was full and fragrant, and now the prickly-pear cactus is gorgeous with waxy yellow flowers. The bougainvillea has finally come into its glory; the bushes look like huge clouds of color—magenta, purple, coral.

We hear that Michigan had its coldest, snowiest winter in several years (where *was* that groundhog?), but Sharon's surviving—likes school and her job. She said she walked outside one morning and thought, Hmmm, feels like it's warming up. And sure enough it was. Right up to 19° (!)

Meanwhile, here at the ranch . . . our Spanish classes turned out to be one of the most fun things we did this winter. I'd been reluctant to ask people to plunk down money for textbooks on a venture that was pretty experimental for me. So I combined ideas from several sources, added my own examples, and created my own handouts. It helped to run my ideas by Howard. (He gets a gold star.)

On my birthday everyone surprised me with song and gift certificates to the Mall in Laredo. I'd had a feeling they were cooking up something, but thought it might be a group trip to El Jacal de Pizza. Well, they had that in mind too—another big surprise, since I didn't know I was entitled to *two* surprises!

Our friend Florence turned seventy-five and had her annual "bus-stop" shindig. This is what some folks would call "happy hour," but there's a story behind the current name. Back in Michigan, Jim and Natalie used to enjoy a before-dinner drink in the late afternoon, but the cocktail hour gradually crept up earlier and earlier. Finally they decided they'd better draw a deadline before it became a before-noon drink, so they agreed to wait until the school bus had made its afternoon stop by their house. Thus the "bus-stop hour" was born. Of course no one around here has kids in school anymore, so we can rearrange the time to suit the occasion.

One of our friends remarked that if you weren't already a bird watcher before coming to South Texas, for sure you'd become one once you got here. Many birds native to Mexico and South America aren't found in any other part of the USA, except in the Rio Grande Valley of Texas, so we consider it a real privilege to see them. The green jays are always a treat to see, with their tropical green, blue, and yellow coloring.

We also like to watch the flat-topped yellow-fronted kiskadee flycatchers, another species unique to this area. Their name has to do with their call, which sounds more like "peek-a-boo" to me. They're very *noisy*, and it sounds like they're scolding each other all the time. (Or just playing peek-a-boo; who knows?)

For a while we had a golden-fronted woodpecker hammering at our palm tree, but I guess it moved on to greener insects. Instead, we have grackles prancing across the roof in search of their own kind of gourmet breakfast (lake flies). Or maybe it's the gourmet breakfast stomping across our roof in search of grackles.

The RV park has had quite a turnover in the last few weeks— Winter Texans moving back home, and young construction workers moving in. One guy set up a bright striped *beach umbrella* on the concrete pad by his trailer (in the middle of the park—nowhere near any kind of a beach) and hauled out his ghetto-blaster to grace us all with a heavy-metal concert one afternoon. But, except for him and the grackles, it's been rather quiet.

GOLIAD, TEXAS—April 13, 1994

We finally pulled out of Zapata. How we enjoyed the prickly pear, lantana, winecups, and other wildflowers along the highway! We traveled 200 miles northeast to a beautiful state park in Goliad, about halfway between Zapata and Houston.

Just as we began setting up, along came an elderly man in a golf-cart asking where we were from. I was more-or-less standing on my head at the time, trying to secure the jacks, but I looked up long enough to say we'd just come from Zapata. So, being in a conversational mood, he asked how many RV parks are there.

I said (still from my upside-down position), "Maybe fifteen or twenty."

He finally got around to asking, "Have you seen the one with the big fish in front?" (referring to a twelve-foot papier-mâché fish in front of the office). When I told him that was where we'd stayed, he said, "My friend made that fish."

Well, that got me upright, and Howard joined us so we could all trade tales of "Julio" and *his* tales. "Julio" is our friend Julius, who at seventy-three is one of the most active enthusiastic people we know. After recovering from heart surgery ten years ago, he began a vigorous exercise program. Last year Howard and Lester joined him for a 1-1/2-mile walk across the bridge to the Dairy Queen at 6:00 every morning. There Julio (who was the inspiration for starting our Spanish class) ordered coffee in Spanish and asked pertinent questions, such as, "*¿Dónde está su elefante?*" for the amusement of the girls who worked behind the counter.

He spoke Spanish whenever he could, around town *and* the park. In the afternoon he frequently rode his bike, stopping to chit-chat with folks about their *esposos, gatos, perros, elefantes,* or *cualquier* (spouses, cats, dogs, elephants, or whatever). He's one of those people: "To know him is to love him."

After chatting with Julio's friend and getting situated, we took in our surroundings. Goliad and the adjacent Presidio La Bahia are rich in history from Spanish colonial times through the Texas Revolution.

The presidio was originally established in 1721 to thwart French encroachment into Texas, which was a Spanish province at that time.

"Goliad" (an anagram for "Hidalgo") was given its name to honor Father Miguel Hidalgo, "the patriot priest of the Mexican Revolution," who roused his countrymen to break free from Spain in 1810 with his famous "Grito de Dolores" (Cry of Dolores).

When General Antonio López de Santa Anna—who called himself "The Napoleon of the West"—came to power in Mexico, his egomania and ruthlessness led to the Texas Revolution. (Even in Mexico, Santa Anna's checkered reign is considered a blot on Mexican history.)

On December 20, 1835, twenty-five years after Mexico proclaimed its independence from Spain, Texas declared its independence from Mexico. The first Declaration of Texas Independence was signed at Presidio La Bahia by ninety-two citizens and distributed throughout the state. Here flew the first flag of Texas Independence.

Two weeks after the end of the siege on the Alamo, Col. James Fannin surrendered his troops to the Mexican Army at Coleto Creek near Goliad. Rather than grant them clemency, as Mexican General Urrea urged, Santa Anna gave orders to execute them. Not trusting Urrea to carry this out, Santa Anna commissioned another officer to do so. Thus, on Palm Sunday, a week later, 341 of Fannin's men were killed at point-blank range.

This was the real turning point in the revolution. Spurred by cries of "Remember Goliad" and "Remember the Alamo," Texans ultimately defeated Santa Anna at San Jacinto less than a month after The Goliad Massacre.

I was touched to learn about one of the little known heroes, rather heroines, of Goliad, Francisca Álvarez. The common-law wife of an officer under General Urrea's command, she came to the aid of wounded Texans throughout the war, with no thought for her own safety. Not only that, but through her compassionate intervention, twenty of Fannin's men were saved from execution. She was known as "the angel of Goliad." (Almost exactly ten years after our visit to Goliad, a statue of Señora Álvarez was erected there, and her rightful place in history is becoming more widely recognized.)

LAFAYETTE, LOUISIANA—April 21-24, 1994

What a fascinating place this town is! They say (whoever "they" are) that southern Louisiana is cosmopolitan, catholic, colorful, and fun-loving. The motto is *Laissez les bon temps rouler*—Let the good times roll.

Lafayette, the "Cajun Capital" of Louisiana, is quite culturally diverse—like Albuquerque, but with its own variety of cultures. We love to hear people speaking Cajun, which seems to be a combination of English, French, and their own lingo.

We had the good fortune of arriving the week of the annual Festival International de Louisiane, a large fair that features culinary, musical, and art exhibits from a number of places linked to French and/or Louisiana traditions. We enjoyed concerts by musicians from such far-reaching parts of the world as Corsica, the Caribbean, and Africa. There was even a group from Ireland that showed how Celtic music influenced, and was influenced by, music from Brittany.

We stayed at the Acadiana City Park. The park ranger, Joe Thibodaux, was friendly and helpful in explaining local customs. He said it was essential to speak French in his job, and told us that on weekends when visitors from both Québec and France arrived (for example), they enjoyed being able to communicate in their common language.

However, it does seem strange, after coming from South Texas, to hear so much French instead of Spanish. So one afternoon while sitting at a restaurant waiting for our meal, we entertained ourselves by speaking Spanish. I asked Howard things like,

"¿Hay un caiman debajo de la mesa?"

(Is there an alligator under the table?)

And he'd answer,

"No, no hay un caiman; hay goom debajo de la mesa."

("Goom" = "gum.")

PASS CHRISTIAN, MISSISSIPPI
April 27 through May 2, 1994

Here we are, a little further along in our journey toward Florida. Lately we've been experiencing what the weathercasters call "shower activity" and what we common folk call "rain."

One day we took a trolley ride, thinking this would be a leisurely way to enjoy the sights. However, instead of taking the "Scenic Drive" slowly, the driver took the busy highway quickly.

We got off at Gulfport and browsed around one of the casinos. Then we trolleyed in the other direction to Bay St. Louis and another casino. By the time we were ready to head home, the shower activity had begun in earnest. Part of the trolley was air-conditioned mechanically and the other part by the open windows. So our choice of seats was either (a) chilly and damp, or (b) chilly and dry. When we came home, the only way to save the day was to bake brownies.

A couple of weeks ago, I decided it was finally safe to plant the herb garden Sharon had given me for my birthday. The directions said to cover it with plastic wrap, and place it in a warm sunny place while the seeds germinated. Even though the weather had suddenly decided to be cold and not sunny, the seedlings started popping up early. So who knows what will happen.

I finally removed the plastic wrap and have the planter on our picnic table here. Now that we're in one of the most jungly places I've ever seen, I feel confident the shower activity, climate, and Mississippi mud (which I'm not sure it's such a treat to beat your feet in) will do wonders.

Sometimes I haven't the foggiest notion what season this is. Last summer I nearly wore out my sweatshirts because it was so cold, and this winter has been mild; so I live in constant confusion about where we're headed next (both travel-wise and season-wise). Traveling to Florida is not a very summer-thing-to-do and contributes to my general fuzziness.

The bon temps have been rolling here too. The beginning of the shrimp season was celebrated this weekend with a big festival, which included the blessing of the fleet.

The other day while I was poking around a bookstore, Howard sat outside watching the seashore. When I came back, he told me he thought a caiman had run across his shoe, but it turned out to be a lizard.

GULF SHORES, ALABAMA—May 3-7, 1994

My cousin Bobby and his wife, Afton, have a condo here on the gulf. They can sit on their balcony, enjoy the breeze, and look out at the beautiful seashore. Now I know why everyone is so enchanted with the Alabama and Florida beaches. This part of the

Gulf Coast, and all along the Florida panhandle, is called "the emerald coast" because of the color of the water (which varies from green to aqua to turquoise to royal blue). The beaches are called "sugar beaches" because the sand is so white and fine.

Up till now, I hadn't known ocean water could be clear and sparkling. Growing up near Galveston, Bobby and I used to think all beaches were supposed to have tan sand and dull tan water. Nevertheless, we've always had a special affinity for the gulf. Now that he's retired, Bobby wants to live out the rest of his life "on the seashore."

Howard and I liked the state park where we stayed—roomy and woodsy. There was a big sign in the office that read,

"DON'T AGGRAVATE THE ALLIGATORS.
This is their home."

Well, believe me, the last thing on our minds was aggravating alligators! As it turned out, we didn't even see any. But our neighbor told us that was because we hadn't looked for them at the right time. He said when you shine a light out over the lake at *night*, you can see their eyes glowing red.

FLORIDA—May 8-24, 1994

We had a wonderful week in Orlando, where we visited our son Steve, who's stationed at the naval base there. He showed us around the base and his particular area, where he deals with damage control. We met some of his friends—most importantly, a delightful young lady named Beth Harris. Beth is also stationed there, working in communications.

From there we went up to St. Augustine. This city, established when Ponce de Leon arrived in fifteen-something-or-other, claims to be the oldest permanent European settlement in the United States. (That distinction is easily disputed, however, depending on which history books you read.) Nevertheless it's a beautiful town with a charming old-world flavor, thanks in part to the Mediterranean-style architecture. We did the tourist stuff—rode the trolley, visited shrines, walked around the old fortress . . . and left some things for next time.

The trolley made several stops, one at "The Fountain of Youth." This was quite tempting, but since it didn't do much for ol' Ponce, we traveled on. (Our trolley driver said she didn't know much about its youth-giving properties, but it would certainly make one regular.)

QUITMAN, GEORGIA—May 25, 1994

We're just over the Florida line, at the edge of a small lake. From one window I can see Howard fishing, and from another, AN ALLIGATOR gliding around, surveying its territory. When the alligator got within a few feet of shore, Howard decided to relocate.

At this park, there's a rule stating (in capital letters),

"DON'T FEED THE ALLIGATORS!"

Who can have any fun? No feeding. No aggravating.

Only six other people are staying at this RV park. One couple we like are Joe and Carmen Martín. They told us a funny story about playing golf near our park. When one of Joe's golf balls went out of bounds into the woods, he (naturally) went to find it. What he found instead was a whole slew of balls bunched up together. He wondered why everyone had just abandoned them, until he saw a cottonmouth snake guarding them!

Like us, the Martíns felt they'd found Shangri-La at this serene unpopulated corner of the world—no noise, no traffic. (Just some alligators, mosquitoes, and snakes—oh well.)

UNADILLA, GEORGIA—May 27-31, 1994

Our next stop was Southern Trails RV Resort in a small town "120 miles south of Atlanta and 120 miles north of the Georgia/Florida border." One of the advantages of traveling south in the summertime: quiet uncrowded RV parks.

By happy coincidence, fate, or whatever, we ran into the Martíns again. Joe told us a*nother* alligator story, an incident they witnessed at their previous stop. (You must think I'm obsessed with alligators—right!) Joe said an alligator swam up to a lady who was fishing, grabbed her float and took off, peeling her line right off the reel. I guess she's lucky it found her less interesting than her float.

PHOENIX RESORT
AT TALKING ROCK CREEK PROPERTIES
CHATSWORTH, GEORGIA
June 1-6, 1994

Finally, there's someplace in this part of the country that I can pronounce (after Apalachicola, Wewahitchka, etc.). Thanks to Alan Jackson, I can say "Chattahoochee," but I'm not sure if I can spell it.

Anyway, that's where we are, in the Chattahoochee National Forest. We'd heard it's relatively cool (emphasis on "relatively") in northern Georgia, so we're planning to spend June in several Coast-to-Coast parks around here, one week at a time. Then we'll head toward the Smokies.

We need a bird *tape* to go with our bird book, so we can identify birds by their songs. There are so many here we've never heard, or heard of, before. Except for roadrunners and a few others, most of the birds I remember from Albuquerque belong to the "little and brown" family.

Here we've discovered whippoorwills. We've never *seen* any because they're nocturnal, but they make a terrible racket. Howard thinks they sound like a malfunctioning car-alarm.

Because they seem mysterious, not appearing till after dark, several superstitions have grown up around them. Mothers have used them as a sort of "boogey-man" to scare their kids into behaving. It's said if you don't wash your feet before going to bed, a whippoorwill might carry you off.

DAHLONEGA, GEORGIA—June 7-13, 1994

From the Withlacoochee Creek to the Coosawattee River to Amicalola Falls and Dahlonega, we just slog from one unpronounceable place to another. I didn't realize how hard I'd been concentrating on figuring out the pronunciation of all the Indian names around here, till I saw a road sign saying, "Congested Area," and found myself mentally pronouncing it, "Conga-stedd Area." (Maybe we were approaching the reservation where the Conga-Stedd nation lives?)

Now, fortunately, we are in a woodsy and *UN*congested area. One afternoon we visited Amicalola Falls State Park, where the Appalachian Trail begins. This was especially interesting to us, since we crossed this trail off and on the last time we were back East.

I love the little town of Dahlonega! The square is full of quaint antique shops, local craft shops, "country" gift shops, and such. There are also lots of shade trees and flowers around the square, which surrounds the Gold Museum.

The museum, originally the Old Courthouse, was built using gold found in the area back in the 1830s. We learned that the first gold rush occurred here in Dahlonega (the Indian word for "gold"), long before the rush in California overshadowed it. The county assayer, Mathew Stephenson, implored people not to abandon the hills of Dahlonega in order to head west. Mark Twain's version of this speech is the origin of the saying, "Thar's gold in them thar hills."

The museum also chronicles the way greed for the gold-rich land on which the gentle Cherokees had always lived was responsible for their shameful relocation and mistreatment on the sad "Trail of Tears."

CLEVELAND, GEORGIA—June 14-20, 1994

Here we are in "the mountains" of Georgia, which don't seem very steep or mountainous to us "Westerners." Wednesday we drove over to the strangely named Hog Pen Gap, where the Appalachian

Trail crosses one of the scenic winding byways. We hiked in for a mile or so, then turned back—just didn't feel like traipsing all the way up to Maine.

Along the trail we saw gorgeous "flame azaleas" (which are peach-colored), "fire-pinks" (which are bright red), and some pretty purple things that I think are called "spiderwort." There were also several million bugs, whose names I don't know—I call them "little hovering things."

We're five miles from Helen, a charming town designed to look Bavarian. Every single business follows the pattern, even the "River Haus Pizza" and the place specializing in Irish memorabilia. The Ace Hardware sports a mural of a bearded man in Alpine attire using some tools.

Saturday night we went to a "Mountain Music Show" nearby, which was fun and informal—I think the entertainers were whoever happened to show up that night. First a bluegrass band played some lively tunes, keeping strict poker faces. We thought it might be in their contract not to smile. Some woman in the audience got up and began clogging in the middle of one of their numbers, and they never blinked an eye.

The audience was maybe ten or fifteen people—it was hard to tell who was audience and who wasn't, because different unlikely people kept getting up to perform. Unfortunately, the music was too loud for a small gathering, so after a few hours our ears were ready to go home.

TALLULAH RIVER MOUNTAIN RESORT TALLULAH FALLS, GEORGIA June 21-27, 1994

The campgrounds just get prettier and prettier. Our site was not only spacious and shady, but right on the Chatooga River. Howard enjoyed fishing outside our back door and all along the bank.

Let me tell you what we desert folk have discovered about humidity: When the humidity is 100%, after a while the air gets so saturated it just starts leaking. At first I confused this with rain, but by the time I'd raced around to close all the windows, it had stopped again, so I've learned not to pay attention.

June 27, 1994

Last night we had some REAL rain. All-night-long, pay-attention-to, heavy rain, with thunder and lightning. We could tell the river had risen just by hearing it roar past us, even before we looked out the window this morning. In some places, the lingering debris indicated where the river had gone over the banks. The churning mud had turned the water the color of red Georgia clay. We saw large branches caught on rocks, and I got an inkling of what the folks on the Mississippi must have felt last summer. Even on our small river, the flood was frightening.

At least we can't complain about the heat—it hasn't gotten over 80° here in the shade. So when we're swept down the Chatooga into the Tugaloo into the Savannah and eventually into the Atlantic Ocean, you can say, "Well, they were a little moldy, but they were cool."

UNICOI STATE PARK, GEORGIA
June 28 through July 5, 1994

And why is Georgia so green? Rain, rain, and more rain in the five-day forecast. And more excitement! Wednesday night about 7:30—shortly after lightning had caused the power to go out—one of the rangers pounded on our door to tell us a tornado had been sighted heading toward the campground and we should go to the lodge for safety. Howard and I each grabbed a book (but not a flashlight to read by) and our raincoats, and left without further ado. People more experienced than we had brought flashlights, pillows, and even sleeping bags. Fortunately, the tornado veered, and we were able to go back home about an hour later.

We learned that the same storm we'd experienced at Tallulah Falls two nights earlier had been even more severe here, and everyone had been rousted out at 2:00 a.m. (!) to go to the lodge for shelter.

We also learned that a path of tornadoes had torn all across northern Georgia on Palm Sunday, killing eighteen people. One of those was an employee at the park where we'd stayed in Dahlonega. Some areas of the park itself were destroyed.

Between Helen and Cleveland, nine miles to the south, the property damage was very disheartening. We saw trees uprooted, buildings demolished, someone's car with a tree smashed across it . . . This all happened recently enough that everyone is still edgy. I don't mean to dwell on disasters, but all this made quite an impression on us.

There are no large cities north of Atlanta, seventy-five miles away. So whenever we look at a TV weather map of Georgia, there's nothing we can relate to. At Chatsworth, we were closer to Chattanooga than any city in Georgia, so we got one (1) station, which gave us Tennessee news and weather. Tallulah Falls is on the South Carolina border, so there we got one (1) station from "the Carolinas," which gave *its* news and weather.

When the weathercaster reported that "Oconee County is under tornado watch," we looked at a South Carolina map and discovered Oconee bordered our county in Georgia. Apparently the tornado came to a screeching halt when it reached the state line, so we were safe after all.

Thursday we took a two-mile hike sponsored by the park. The day looked a little gray, which might have scared folks off, because there were only four of us, including the park ranger, Eric, and another visitor, David. We had a good time, congenial company, and new things to discover.

Eric showed us how to squeeze juice from the jewel plant to produce an antidote to poison ivy. We were glad we didn't need to test the theory, however. We never knew there were so many varieties of 'shrooms—and so colorful. We also learned which ones were poisonous (all of them, I think). So instead of sampling mushrooms, we all chewed some *sour*wood leaves.

Storms notwithstanding, Georgia should really be named "Gorgeous" (if they'd just shift a few letters around and add/subtract some). Our six weeks here have gone by quickly, and we'd love to come back in the spring or fall to see the changing seasons.

KNOXVILLE, TENNESSEE—July 20-24, 1994
WEIRD ADVENTURE #3219

The week before coming here, we stayed at a *very noisy* RV park in North Carolina. We spent each night listening to the roar of eighteen-wheelers zooming down the highway, which seemed to run through our back yard.

So, more than ever, we were happy to find a *quiet* park off the highway near Knoxville. But our peace was shattered the very first night. We were enjoying a sound sleep when suddenly—about 1:00 in the morning—someone started banging on our door.

My first fuzzy thought: "Oh no, where is the tornado?" The next thought: "I'm too sleepy to get up and relocate."

Howard answered the pounding. It was our fifty-something neighbor from across the street (I'll call him "Coo-Coo"), who informed Howard that "someone just hit your trailer!"

My mind rejected this because we'd been hit before, and I know how that feels. We hadn't felt anything. Coo-Coo went on to explain that we'd been hit by a *rock*, that some troublemakers had been throwing rocks at him and his wife and had hit us by mistake. Howard went out with a flashlight and found the windshield of our truck smashed.

Coo-Coo said he could identify the vandals and was insistent that Howard call the police. Coo-Coo's wife (I'll call her "Dizzy") accompanied Howard to the pay phone, explaining that he shouldn't walk down alone, there were a lot of Crazy People in the park. Little did we know she was one of them.

It did seem odd to me, even in my sleepy state, that they were so anxious to get the police involved. Coo-Coo's agitation seemed out of proportion to someone else's broken windshield. And though I wasn't happy about the windshield, I pictured twelve-year-old boys throwing rocks, yielding to that mysterious magnetism between the two. Couldn't this wait till the light of day? Why was Coo-Coo talking so loud, and where were all the other people he'd surely wakened?

The managers—very sane and pleasant people—showed up, took Howard aside, and shed light on the situation. They'd been trying for months to evict Coo-Coo and Dizzy, but hadn't been successful because the couple had children living at home with them. Their only occupation was suing people, and they hadn't paid rent in months. Their first and only payment had been supplied by checks from four different churches they'd conned into feeling sorry for them. This latest adventure was an attempt by Coo-Coo and Dizzy to retaliate against some park employees for imagined insults.

The police came; the report got made; we went back to bed but not so readily to sleep. Howard and I speculated that Coo-Coo might have even thrown the rocks himself, then rejected the idea. Surely a middle-aged RVer wouldn't do such a childish thing!

Next morning the police returned, and this time all the neighbors *were* out and milling around. Sure enough, our speculations were right on target. Our next-door neighbor Betty had been unable to sleep and had seen Coo-Coo throw the rock that hit our windshield. Evidently everyone else (but us) knew that Coo-Coo and Dizzy were nuts and were leery of confronting them in the middle of the night.

What happened next was like something out of a slapstick movie. A policeman knocked on Coo-Coo's door and had to wait a few minutes for him to don his neck-brace before coming outside. The neck-brace was another thing that had given rise to neighborhood gossip. Coo-Coo had been seen working on his car (the only work he'd ever been seen doing, apparently) with no sign of injury or impairment. The neck-brace was for the benefit of whichever people or institutions he happened to be suing at the moment.

While this was hardly the ideal way to meet the *rest* of our neighbors, it certainly broke the ice. One neighbor, a friendly "South Texican," as he called himself, hauled out his video camera and aimed it at the action, all the while giving a monologue to explain the events. He turned to us at one point and whispered with a mischievous grin, "There's not any film in here, but they don't know that." Then he whipped around to focus on the Coo-Coos again, resuming his late-news-TV-reporter role.

I suspect this play-acting was helpful in the long run. The Coo-Coos had committed a few other acts of vandalism during the night, so perhaps they began to wonder how damaging the non-existent video might be.

After all this, Howard and I, together with our next-door neighbors, spent the rest of the morning at the Knox County courthouse with our harassed manager, while he patiently tried to cut through the red tape of pressing charges.

Whatever motivated them, and despite efforts of the misguided church people to let them stay, the Coo-Coos decided to leave that same day. That night the park threw a "Ding Dong the Witch Is Dead" party to celebrate. There we met a number of friendly people—the kind of RVers we're *accustomed* to meeting—and enjoyed a peaceful stay from then on.

OTHER WEIRD ADVENTURES—Summer 1994

We had some strange on-the-road experiences having to do with religious fanatics. At one park in Florida, our neighbors had big posters in every window with Bible quotations (taken out of context, of course). One was "Your sin will find you out!" A friendly way to introduce themselves, I suppose. Actually, they seemed pretty nice, the few times they ventured out of their poster-darkened trailer—didn't even comment on our sins.

Many of the RV parks have non-denominational church services, which—up till now—we had always enjoyed. These usually included several songs and a few words of prayer and inspiration. Well, we were in for something new at one park in North Carolina.

The service was held outdoors, under a pavilion, which turned out to be a good thing. We sang only two songs; then the preacher launched into a sermon that went on and on and on and on and on. I'm not exactly sure what he said, except for telling us that *sinners* didn't like to see him coming and often got up and left mid-sermon.

I got more caught up in his cadence—something like a tobacco auctioneer's—than his actual words. Rat-a-tat-rat-a-tat-rat-a-tat.

After an hour, I slipped out quietly, no doubt "proving" myself the kind of sinner he'd referred to earlier. Shortly afterwards (according to Howard, who bravely stayed on), a motorhome stopped alongside the pavilion for several minutes. The driver was someone who enjoyed the roar of his diesel, so the sound effectively drowned out the preacher, who finally quit trying to compete.

Although somewhat shell-shocked by the whole episode, Howard and I haven't given up on trying park-sponsored services in the future.

APPOMATTOX COURT HOUSE, VIRGINIA
July 30 through August 1, 1994

I don't think we expected to get so caught up in Civil War history. But our route took a turn when Howard thought since we were in this part of the country, we might as well visit some battlefields.

Our itinerary had more to do with the location of Coast to Coast parks than with Civil War sites, which is why Appomattox Court House was our first stop rather than our last. One thing we learned is that the county seats in Virginia were named Something-or-Other *Court House* at one time, which was rather confusing at first.

So Lee's surrender to Grant did not take place in the courthouse building at Appomattox—which would have seemed logical—but rather at Mr. McLean's *farmhouse* in the town of Appomattox Court House.

Poor ol' Mr. McLean. The war had practically begun on the lawn of his former home in Manassas. So he'd picked up and moved his family away from there—away from all the fighting—to the quiet peaceful village of Appomattox C.H., where he thought they'd be out of harm's way for the duration of the war.

However, the *last* battles were fought practically at his doorstep too. I'm not sure he was too happy about having his home chosen as the place for the two generals to meet, but somehow that seemed to be the most suitable place in town.

There were, so we hear, 10,000 battles fought in this war, and it seems that wherever one occurred, the people who live there now say their site was *the* most significant. They all have fascinating tales to tell, but they're obviously not of equal importance in the overall scheme of things. (Don't tell the residents of these 10,000+ towns.)

Apparently the sites that are *really* most crucial have been set aside by the National Park Service, which does a great job providing interpretive tours, videos, "living history" talks, displays, etc. "Living History" is well named—the actors certainly make the events come alive. Park Ranger Jim Cooke, as "Corporal Cooke of Pennsylvania," held us spellbound with his account of what happened at Appomattox C.H.

People could ask questions, but had to keep them in the context of 1865. He never got out of character—remarked to Howard that he must have been to France to have a *wrist*watch, since those hadn't reached the US yet. People could also ask to take his "image" (photo), which we did.

We spent another afternoon at Sayler's Creek up the road, where the last battle of Lee's campaign was actually fought. This isn't one of the more touristy spots, consisting mostly of rolling farmland and a small stone house that was closed to the public.

We were the only ones there that day. While we were wandering around looking at historical markers, someone from the preservation committee showed up to mow the lawn. When he asked if we'd like to see inside the house, we jumped at the chance to take our own private tour. The house itself was rather plain, but we were fascinated to hear how it had once served as a hospital—just as most houses back then were used.

FRONT ROYAL, VIRGINIA
August 9-14, 1994

We visited "Belle Boyd's Cottage" one afternoon. Front Royal's claim to fame is that Stonewall Jackson captured the town from the Union thanks to the efforts of a feisty Confederate spy named

Belle Boyd. (The town changed hands many times afterwards, so this victory was short-lived.)

Now Belle was a very unconventional and headstrong young lady. Once when her parents denied her permission to go to a party, she went anyway, riding her horse right through the parlor! (Oh, these teenagers!)

During and after the war, to make ends meet, she went on stage, where she gave monologues describing her exploits as a spy. I'm not sure which was more shocking in that era—being a spy, or going on stage.

Before visiting her home, now a fascinating museum, we knew nothing about Belle or this town except that it was en route to Gettysburg.

We didn't even realize that Front Royal was at the entrance to Shenandoah National Park. Didn't even know there *was* a Shenandoah National Park. (No more rock-throwing at people who don't know there's a NEW Mexico.) Yesterday we explored the northern end of the park, where the dogwood was in full bloom, resembling large puffs of pink or white cotton candy.

Another day we went up to Winchester, a few miles from here. Winchester—naturally—considers itself the most strategically located place on the Civil War map. It changed hands over seventy times—thirteen times in one day alone. Like most of Virginia, it is rich in both Civil War and Colonial history and landmarks. It's also the home of Patsy Cline. (Yes, it's a little surreal to drive down Patsy Cline Blvd. on the way to George Washington's office or Stonewall Jackson's headquarters.)

But that's not the reason we went. From some research my Tennessee cousin Emma Lee had done, we believed our great-great-grandfather, Martin Gibson, had been captured at Winchester. As it turned out, we were mistaken, which we learned in a rather roundabout way.

Earlier, while in Fredericksburg, we met one of the park ranger-historians, Eric Mink, who impressed us with his knowledge and overall helpfulness. Eric not only answered our questions, but gave us quite a bit of history that we wouldn't have learned otherwise.

It was nice to find someone so willing to go the extra mile and fill us in on all these interesting sidelights.

We ran into him again at another site where he'd been assigned for the day, and again he seemed to have all the time in the world for us. This time we got into a conversation about ancestors. We told him about our difficulties tracing family members when they'd fought on different sides of the Mason-Dixon line and weren't speaking to one another afterwards.

Eric said *his* Confederate ancestor no one in the family would talk about had not only turned himself in to the Union Army, but had had the audacity to move to *Philadelphia*! (Horrors!) Then Eric said, "Anyone can have an ancestor who's a hero. But not everyone will claim a black sheep."

I think Eric brought up this story because he'd looked up someone's ancestor who was supposed to be a hot-shot and turned out to be a deserter. He said people don't take too kindly to having their family legends overturned.

He offered to look up Martin Gibson for us and probably wanted to be sure we wouldn't hold him personally responsible if Martin didn't turn out to be such a good guy.

This was several weeks ago, and I'd almost forgotten about it when I got a letter from Dennis Pfranz of the Park Service in Fredericksburg, regarding Eric's research. He told us that Emma Lee had gotten Martin Gibson's record confused with someone else's. He went on to tell us, in a very tactful way, of Martin's actual service.

The letter said in part, "Gibson enlisted in the 21st [North Carolina] regiment at the age of 58, but was discharged just ten weeks later . . . . The rigor of army life, it seems, was too much for a man of his advanced years."

I found this explanation rather funny, since I had reached that advanced year myself. In retrospect, it seemed quite reasonable—I've always marveled at *anyone* who survived the entire war, and especially, I admit it, someone of Martin's advanced years. Personally, I think it made more sense to get out of the war than to stay in.

On my mother's side of the family, she says that her (Yankee) grandfather claimed he was too OLD to be in the army, so—after serving a couple of months—went back home to the farm. He said that "somebody has to stay home and look after the womenfolk and children." When I looked him up in our family records, I saw that he was only twenty-two years old when the war began.

Whenever I tell my mother this, however, she looks surprised and says, "Hmm, isn't that something!" Then the next time she tells the story, she tells it exactly the way she's always told it.

GETTYSBURG, PENNSYLVANIA
August 20-26, 1994

"THE WORLD WILL LITTLE NOTE,
NOR LONG REMEMBER,
WHAT WE SAY HERE,
BUT IT CAN NEVER FORGET
WHAT THEY DID HERE."

Abraham Lincoln

Being in Gettysburg again was the high point of our Civil War journey. This place has quite an emotional impact on us. On our guided tour of the National Cemetery, the ranger spoke with great feeling about the timelessness of the words of the Gettysburg Address. He suggested that we read it again while we were here.

The Address is engraved on a monument honoring Lincoln, and later I noticed two teenage boys from our group studying the inscription. I was glad to see they'd taken the ranger's words to heart. It was also good to be reminded that there are lots of thoughtful teenagers out there. Howard and I have both been impressed with the intelligent questions asked by the kids in our various groups.

When I was in school, I thought there were only two generals involved—Lee and Grant—and still have trouble sorting out all the other names. So when we read inscriptions that say, "As the enemy approached . . . ," we not only have to figure out which name belongs to which army, but also have to remember which side of the Mason-Dixon line we're visiting.

Since the plaques were made long after the war, long past the point of referring to our fellow countrymen—on either side—as "the enemy," I think the armies should be identified as either Union or Confederate.

ON THE ROAD AGAIN—September, 1994

After finishing our battlefield tours, we had originally hoped to come to Albuquerque for a month. However none of the places we called would make reservations because of the upcoming Balloon Fiesta. This time of year they can charge *daily* rates for a higher fee. Maybe if we come during dust-storm season, no one will be battling over RV sites and they'll pay us instead.

So we had the unexpected pleasure of discovering several CCC parks in Pennsylvania and New York while waiting for our family revolution (excuse me, *reunion*) that's taking place in October.

We did spend one week in a rather strange RV park. Actually it was very pretty, with lots of trees, and grass so green it looked like a carpet. The park was spacious and uncrowded; there were about 200 sites, but only thirty RVs. So here's the strange part: The manager had a few favorite spaces he loved to keep filled, so all thirty of us were bunched together. In fact, three of us were lined up *lengthwise*, like a freight train. When it was time to leave, we were afraid we might have to wiggle out sideways. But with Howard's skillful maneuvering, we exited the usual way.

OSSINING, NEW YORK—October 3-14, 1994

At last the time arrived for our family reunion. My kids had been talking for years about "spending Thanksgiving with Aunt Louise," and it came as something of a surprise when I found they'd actually made concrete plans. Louise thinks she invited them, and Bill thinks *he* invited them, so that's good, because I thought we'd all just invited ourselves.

The end of November is a little "iffy" for traveling—airlines booked, weather unpredictable, etc. So we/they decided an earlier date would be wiser. And since the Canadians are considerate enough to celebrate their Thanksgiving early in October, we decided to celebrate along with them. This is our favorite time of year, no matter where we are.

Throughout the week we had fun hiking around town, enjoying the changing colors of the leaves, and sightseeing in New York City and at West Point. On Thanksgiving Day itself (October 10th), we were able to use the parish hall of the Episcopal Church Louise and Bill attend, which provided ample room for our large extended families. We all agreed our vacation was a huge success.

ZAPATA, TEXAS
October 31 through December 31, 1994

December 7, 1994

"It's beginning to feel a lot like summer!" Would you believe the temperature hit 91 degrees yesterday? We tied Laredo for the nation's hot spot. So much for chestnuts roasting . . . . (South Texans, maybe, but not chestnuts.)

We like our new location this year, just down the road from our old Bass Lake neighborhood. Some friends from Bass Lake— Edna and Jerry Woodard—bought some lakefront property and started a small RV park over the summer months. There's a total of eight (roomy) sites, plus a rec room, boat ramp, and dock.

All the residents (six couples right now) consider it "home," and are busy landscaping, etc. It's the "etc." that's work, but it's gratifying to see the results. So far we've put up storage sheds (like an Amish barnraising, with everyone pitching in), and some stepping stones.

The park is called "Veleño View" because it's situated on the Veleño branch of the Rio Grande (or more accurately, Falcon Lake). Right now the lake is way down from last year, which was way down from the year before. If and when it comes up again, the lake will be right to the edge of our park.

Even now we have a nice view, and especially like watching the moonrise over the water. There's a huge mesquite tree between our place and the Woodards, where the green jays like to fly in and out. In the mesa down the road lives a family of cardinals; they stay pretty well hidden in the brush, but occasionally we see a flash of red.

We've started Spanish classes again, entertaining ourselves by learning useful phrases. For example, the last class focused on "¿Dónde Está?" The assignment was for all the wives to learn to ask, "Where are the keys?" and the husbands to learn, "They're in your purse."

December 22, 1994

Good news! Howard and Bill Flowers went fishing by Falcon Dam all day yesterday, and between them they caught three dam fish! The weather was gorgeous, and they enjoyed goofing off—pardon me, struggling to capture food for our table.

Well, yesterday was winter, so they say. Yessiree—that mercury plunged all the way down to 75° by midday. So much for winter.

Howard and I decided our Christmas present to each other would be our weekend in San Antonio—and what a wonderful present it turned out to be! It has always been one of my favorite cities, but Howard had never been there. So when the Woodards suggested we all go to the Symphony Pops Christmas concert, it seemed like a perfect opportunity.

I'm embarrassed to say that, up till now, my memory of Texas history/geography centered around a relief map of Texas made out of a salt/flour mixture by our third-grade class when we lived in Houston. We painted it various colors according to its geological features. The area around Houston and east Texas was flat and green; the central area, flat and yellow; El Paso and the Big Bend, brown and lumpy. For some reason I remembered this much more clearly than the events at the Alamo.

But visiting the Alamo, and remembering our recent visit to Goliad, we became immersed in the complexity of Texas history. We found ourselves wondering, as we did while visiting Civil War sites, how the course of history—and consequently our own lives—would have changed if even one circumstance had been altered. The Alamo hero Bowie, for example, was once intensely loyal to Mexico, and would probably never have pushed for Texas independence if Santa Anna hadn't become such a cruel dictator. So many "what ifs."

These events reminded me of Howard's ancestors on the Russian-Polish border, not knowing which flag would fly over their city from one day to the next. It must have been like that at one time here in Texas. One day you were a Spanish colonist; the next, a Mexican citizen; then a citizen of the Republic of Texas; then an American citizen; next a Confederate citizen; then an American once again. In Zapata, fourteen flags were flown at one time or another.

In the plaza by the Alamo we saw a tall tree decorated with big colorful piñatas. We also enjoyed watching a small group of young women doing some Old English folk dances. The next day at the Mercado we listened to a group of Peruvian pan pipers from the Andes.

One of the highlights of our trip was simply walking along the River Walk and taking in all the lights and decorations. Another was the concert, our enticement for coming in the first place.

Something else that turned out to be fun was looking at the extravagant window display at Dillard's. In each window was a different life-size scene from *The Nutcracker*. Howard said it reminded him of when he was a little boy in Chicago, and his mother would take him downtown during the holidays to look at the lavish store displays—especially in elegant places like Marshall Fields.

1995

ZAPATA, TEXAS
January 1 through April 1, 1995

January 23, 1995

We used to chuckle at our neighbors Frank and Helen, who'd spend the first few months they were here moving in, and the last few months moving out. I think it's their turn to laugh. We still haven't started on projects we had in mind when we came down; however, we *have* filled our storage shed to "overload" capacity. I don't know how we found room in our RV for all that stuff in the first place, so it'll probably take us till April to cram it back in again.

I flew out to Phoenix over the holidays. One of my favorite "treasures of the heart" was watching our granddaughters Margot and Adrienne playing at the park without a care in the world, laughing together on a tire-swing.

From there I flew to Corpus. Howard drove over from Zapata, and we flew to Cincinnati for Steve and Beth's wedding. The warm welcome we got from Beth and her family offset the cold and snow outside.

On the way back to Zapata afterwards, something happened that reminded us of why we like our laid-back little community so much. We were about five miles from town when we found the highway blocked by the sheriff's squad car, its lights flashing. We immediately thought that some disaster had occurred.

However we soon saw the cause for alarm. Somebody's cow had wandered out onto the road—which certainly could have caused a serious *problema*—and the sheriff was edging it off the road and back to where it belonged. It was refreshing to know that this was the biggest "crime" of the day.

ON THE ROAD—April 2 through July 12, 1995

After leaving Zapata, we stayed one night in Del Rio. Our next stop was Langtry, where the colorful Judge Roy Bean, *The Law West of the Pecos*, once exercised his unique brand of justice. According to frontier lore, "West of the Pecos, there is no law; west of El Paso, there is no God"—that is, until Judge Bean came along. It's also said that his motto was, "Hang 'em first; try 'em later," but there's no record that he ever ordered anyone to be hanged.

Judge Bean claimed to have named the town for his idol, English actress Lillie Langtry (although there are less romantic explanations for the town's name). Judge Bean's version captures the imagination, however, and the Jersey Lily Saloon still stands as a testament to his admiration for this lady. Having received so many fan letters from Judge Bean over the years, Miss Langtry finally visited the town, although, sadly, it wasn't until after his death.

From Langtry we went to Big Bend National Park. I think we'd need to spend several weeks to see all the sights there. And that doesn't even include all the birdwatching.

We were welcomed to our campsite by a few hundred turkey vultures. They're so huge and ugly, it was a little unnerving to see them right there on and around our picnic table. Once they figured out we didn't have any road kill to share (and evidently didn't look too appetizing ourselves), they flapped off to inspect other campsites.

We also saw some vermilion flycatchers, which should be called vermilion *eyecatchers*. They're bright red and strikingly beautiful. A little grayish bird was quite taken with the mirror on our truck. We couldn't identify it but decided it might be a female of the species. We asked a couple who looked like serious birders what they thought, and they weren't sure either.

The lady said, "Females can be difficult to deal with."

Her husband said to Howard, "See? They even admit it themselves!"

We were camped just a few miles from the Rio Grande (can't get away from it). One of the fascinating things we did was cross the river to the little village of Boquillas, Coahuila (population: 25 families). The river wasn't very wide, and we were ferried across in a little tin rowboat with three other people. Once across, visitors have a choice of riding a burro or a horse, or walking the mile into the village; Howard and I opted to walk.

This was a poor village, but the cute little girls who came up to sell us friendship bracelets were scrubbed clean, with shiny braids and bright hair ribbons.

At the outdoor café, we enjoyed delicious tacos and burritos. I bought a brightly embroidered dress for my mother at the only shop in town. There I heard the owner conversing with other customers, so I told him, "I'm sure your English is much better than my Spanish, pero me gusta practicar (but I like to practice)."

His face lit up, and he was pleased to continue our conversation in Spanish (or I should say "Tex-Mex" on my part). He asked me, "¿Cómo se llama?" And I told him, "Me llamo Margarita." So he told me, "Me llamo José." (So far, so good.)

A few minutes later, Howard came in, and José said, "¿Blah, blah, blah, su esposo, blah, blah, blah?" And I answered,

"Sí."

I hope José was sufficiently impressed with my grasp of the language.

The next day we took a hike to the hot springs. Along the trail were several interesting pictographs from early Indian times. At one point, we saw a marker that asked, "What will *your* children see here in the future?" It went on to say that we need to protect the park from graffiti and vandalism.

For some reason this brought to mind an incident that happened last summer at Gettysburg. The restroom where I stopped was clean and totally graffiti-free, except for an inscription in the stall that read,

CONNIE JONES "74" WAS HERE

Having nothing better to occupy my mind for the time being, I pondered the meaning of "74." Was this Connie's age? Her waist measurement? Her I.Q.? The year she graduated high school? Reform school? Isn't Connie a little old to go around scribbling on walls? (Back to the I.Q. question.)

I'll tell you something. If I ever run across Connie autographing the stalls in some restroom while I'm outside the door doing a little "Hurry-up" dance, I'll break her little crayons.

Well, enough of this philosophical discourse . . . .

*   *   *

Believe it or not, we were *freezing* the first week we got to Phoenix—temperatures 20° below normal. At the same time, temps in Laredo were about 20° *above* normal. (I've lost hope of ever being normal.)

Before coming here, we spent a tranquil week at Twin Lakes Ranch in St. David, Arizona, and attended Easter services at the nearby monastery. The town is small and friendly; the campground attractive; and the monastery peaceful, surrounded by trees and vegetation native to the area. We always find it an ideal place to get our bearings—an essential break from big-city craziness.

After leaving Arizona, we spent time in New Mexico before traveling through Colorado. Besides enjoying the weather, wildflowers, and scenery in general, we made some exciting trips to WalMart. One store in particular had an unusual layout. I found computer supplies on the same aisle with the pots and pans (naturally). After much searching, I finally found some picture frames I'd been looking for. Howard asked me where, and was a little startled when I told him: right by the enema apparatus (of course). The mats for said picture frames weren't anywhere near the frames and corresponding supplies. Instead, they were diagonally across the store, in the farthest corner possible (by the shoe polish, incidentally). All this makes shopping a true adventure.

GRAND TETONS NATIONAL PARK
July 13-16, 1995

When we first told our friend Julio we were going to Big Bend, he asked us, "Why? There's nothing there but *scenery*." That pretty much describes our travels through Rocky Mountain National Park and the Grand Tetons as well. We've certainly been soaking in the gorgeous surroundings.

But even better, we finally caught up with Sharon last week at Jackson Lake Lodge, where she's working. I'd started to get worried because I'd called the employees' dorm for five days in a row without any answer. The only information I got from the switchboard people was, "No one is answering." (Duh.) It turned out that someone had jerked the phone off the wall, which explained a lot.

We finally tracked Sharon down in the Mural Room, and once again marveled at the view of the Tetons through the windows along one wall. After she got off work, Sharon, Howard, and I took a hike along the river, where we nearly bumped into a couple of moose (meese?). Sharon said not to look them in the eye, as moose can be even more dangerous than grizzlies when provoked. The male moose can easily weigh 1200 pounds. And mother bears can't hold a candle to mother moose when it comes to protecting their young. I'm happy to say those we saw were too busy munching underwater goodies to notice us.

I want to pass along a little tidbit I read in the Casper newspaper. It said President Clinton and his family are planning to vacation in the Tetons sometime in August and they are looking forward to "trails, walking, biking, golfing with the wildlife . . . ." From then on, we kept on the lookout for any forms of wildlife playing golf, but were unsuccessful. Guess they play with the Country Club crowd.

Another day Sharon took us hiking through Paintbrush Canyon, where there were a number of colorful flowers. The Indian paintbrush coming into bloom was a bright splashy scarlet. The lupines up here are tall and spindly—more lavender than blue—quite different from their bluebonnet cousins, which are short with dense blossoms and a deep indigo color.

SOUTHSIDE RV PARK, DILLON, MONTANA
July 17 through August 17, 1995

Dillon is one of the prettiest little towns we've come across, and a nice place to take walks. The town has lots of picturesque Victorian homes, each with lush yards, gigantic evergreens, and one or more cats who sit on their respective porches and watch passersby. There's also a colorful variety of flowers—delphinium, poppies, pansies, and petunias are favorites. Summers are so short here, everyone takes full advantage of the growing season.

The RV park is nice too, kind of a mom-n-pop operation—attractive and well-maintained.

The first Sunday we were here, Howard went fishing, and I decided to walk to "a" church. They're all within walking distance. Which one? Eenie meenie miney mo. I decided to try for the Episcopal first, since it had the earliest service. (How's that for spiritual motivation!) It supposedly started at 10:30, but when I got there, the sign said 10:45, and the door was still locked. No cars in sight. No cars by the Methodist Church. No cars anywhere. Had I spaced out a day? Was it indeed Sunday? Was I still on this planet?

Eventually a few people arrived. "Where is Mary?" they asked. No one seemed to know. Then someone named Jane showed up with a key and let us in.

Finally—just as I was wondering if it would be cricket (now that I'd signed the guest book) to erase my name and scoot over to the Methodist Church—someone tootled up in an old red pickup. She was fiftyish, plump, with short gray hair. She was dressed very casually, wearing a floppy fisherman's hat and huge magenta-rimmed sunglasses. It took me a couple of minutes to realize this was the priest, the person we'd been waiting for. This was Mary.

By now it was after 11:00. So much for my "let's-get-to-the-earliest-service" mentality. Mary apologized for being so late—there was a cattle drive between here and Sheridan (her other parish) that she hadn't expected. She disappeared again to put on her vestments, and I was thinking, Next Sunday, the Methodists.

Well, to shorten this long saga, I'm glad I stayed. The whole service was uplifting. Jane had brought cake and coffee, which all twenty of us shared afterwards, and it was a nice chance to get acquainted. By the time I left, I felt quite at home and looked forward to returning.

Sharon and her fiancé, Tom, stopped here on their way to West Virginia, where they'll be working at a resort in Snowshoe. Now you might be thinking that just because West Virginia has "west" in its name, they got confused after leaving Wyoming, headed in the opposite direction, and landed in Montana by mistake. But they had decided to visit both Glacier Park *and* us "between jobs," and we were delighted to have them.

We wanted to show off some of the special sights around town, so first we took them to "Gracie's." Gracie's is a junk yard/shop par excellence. I mean, we have *never* seen such junk as hers, nor are we likely to again in this lifetime.

The shop is dark and cluttered with everything imaginable. In one corner is a barrel full of well-worn mismatched shoes and boots. The boots look as if someone slogged in there through the mud, took off one or both of them, and chucked them into the barrel.

After this, any other activity might seem anticlimactic, but we did enjoy ourselves celebrating Sharon's birthday with a cookout. The cookout featured hamburgers, since Tom and Howard's fishing trip hadn't produced anything but a sunburn. Sharon and I avoided sunburn by staying home to watch "Designing Women" videos and eat cinnamon rolls.

Somehow, in the heat of all this excitement, Howard couldn't find one of his sandals. Tom suggested we return to Gracie's where it had probably already made its way to "the barrel" and he could no doubt buy it back for $1.50. Luckily, we found it under the porch step instead.

Dillon, as you've probably figured out by now, is pretty low-key. There aren't even any traffic lights, probably because there isn't any traffic to speak of. Now some folks might interpret "low-key" as "boring," but how can it be boring when we manage to stumble onto so many fascinating adventures?

One Saturday and Sunday the town featured "Crazy Days," during which several stores held sidewalk sales. We saw some activity in the town park, and mistakenly thought it might be an Arts and Crafts Fair. We discovered as we ambled through the park that we'd inadvertently wandered into a large family reunion!

The reunion planners had set up a huge board with several lists of family trees. At the head of one family was someone who happened to be my ancestor too. A lady who noticed me examining the board said we must be related. Next thing we knew, she had name tags made out for Howard and me.

We hung around for a while, chatting with some of our new-found relatives, then moseyed back into town to take in the "sales" (still wearing the nametags we'd forgotten to remove). Those sales usually feature things they can't get rid of, like oddly sized shoes (which will no doubt wind up at Gracie's) and boring books. But it's fun to look.

ALBUQUERQUE, NEW MEXICO
August 21 through September 28, 1995

We left Dillon on August 17, heading for Gunnison. When we arrived in Green River, Utah, on the 19th, we had an emergency message from Howard's children that their mother had died unexpectedly, the result of a massive stroke. She was only fifty-nine. It was quite a shock, and especially devastating for the kids as well as JoAnn's parents.

So we headed for Albuquerque to help out in whatever way we could. Greg and Diane live in town, Suzanne flew in from Hawaii, Steve and Beth from Florida.

JoAnn had a small drapery shop, and we spent a couple of weeks helping the kids sort through things to be sold or given to friends or charities. It was a strange time, because, sad as it was, we all grew closer, and Howard and I were proud of the way the kids were able to manage such a difficult task.

From one end of the emotional spectrum to the other: On September 9, Mike and Norma were married in a beautiful outdoor ceremony, the weather suddenly and kindly cooperating (after two days of thunderstorms). Not only did we gain a lovely daughter-in-law, but two sweet grandchildren, Kenneth and Celina Baca, seven and six years old, respectively.

From there we made plans to go to Phoenix. Linda called to make a reservation at a mobile home park we like and asked if there'd be space for us October 1. The lady said sorry, but that's when all the snowbirds would be coming down and there wouldn't be anything available. Linda then said we were actually coming September 30, and the lady said, oh, in that case, there'd be plenty of room.

ARIZONA
September 30 through November 1, 1995

Our trip to Phoenix was a see-saw of highs and lows. It's hard to get a handle on my mother's condition. Her short-term memory is pretty bad. (So is mine, so I wonder, "How bad is bad?") Because she's lucid and can enjoy conversing about past events, it's easy to conceal her memory loss.

At least Mom knows who she is and who we are. Also on the plus side, she hasn't lost her sense of humor, and she's still able to take care of her personal needs.

On the minus side, right before we left Phoenix, something very disturbing happened. A sweet-young-thing (syt) came to the door one afternoon and gave Mom a sob-story about needing $10.00, which Mom gave her. Then the syt commented on what a nice house Mom had, so Mom offered to show her around (during which time, Mom's billfold, of course, mysteriously disappeared).

I was so upset when it all came out, and found myself scolding her as if she were a child. "Now you know why Louise and I wish you were living someplace safer . . . ." I really don't like this role-reversal at all.

We called the credit-card company and the police. The policeman who came over to make the report was so nice. We sat around the kitchen table, and Mom asked if he wanted to talk louder or if she should go get her hearing aids.

He said, "Oh, I'll talk louder. I know those things are a nuisance—my grandmother doesn't like to wear them either."

Mom's eyesight is even worse than her hearing, which probably accounts for all the discrepancies in her description of the sweet-young-thing. The syt was "probably white." She was "about Linda's age," Mom said. "Twentyish." (Linda is thirty-five.)

Next, she was "about Linda's size." So I said she must be petite. "Oh, no." Heavy then? No, not heavy either. But short. Then she was "about Teddy's height." Her neighbor Teddy is tall. So we were left to wonder if the young slim white woman my mother described might actually be an elderly fat black man.

Another humorous aspect to this (which, like the other one, only seemed funny a few days later): When the policeman asked Mom how much she weighed, she said, "Well, I don't know," and disappeared. Moments later she returned, toting her bathroom scales.

After she'd weighed herself and had Howard read the numbers, the policeman said cheerfully, "Well, I see you're fit as a fiddle!"

I think Mom couldn't really believe the syt would steal from her. We were also upset that the syt might have told her lunatic boyfriend (as Linda put it) the layout of the house. So all we could do was try to make it more secure for the future. Howard installed sensor lights, as well as an intercom by the back door. I think by now Mom realizes how serious it is (if only she remembers).

We left Phoenix on Halloween and went to St. David, Arizona, where we got together with friends from Zapata. We ate out at a place called "Reb's," where they had country cookin' and country "music" (a quartet of old folks, some of whom played in tune). It was fun; they played mostly old favorites, and we sang along (Bob very loudly, which could only help).

ZAPATA, TEXAS
November 9 through December 31, 1995

A few things are unchanged. The elderly man who drives the yellow lowrider with bright red flames painted on the side is still tooling around town according to his own set of rules (which means not stopping for stop signs or being confined to one particular lane of traffic).

One noticeable change: The lake in our little neck of the arroyo has disappeared entirely.

We haven't seen any green jays yet, but we're glad to find the kiskadees still playing peek-a-boo with each another. And of course it's always good to see old friends again.

1996

January through May, 1996

Much has happened in the last few months. My mother broke her hip the end of January. She underwent a partial hip replacement, then spent February at a rehab center learning to walk again. I was in Phoenix for a couple of weeks, then returned to Zapata, confident that Mom was in good hands—not only with the health care people, but with my daughter Linda to keep an eye on everything.

My sister Louise spent the month of March in Phoenix, searching for just the right intermediate-care place for Mom. The group home Louise found is truly a home. The four ladies who live there are all women who need extra assistance in "everyday" things, but at least—from Mom's point of view—"they have all their marbles."

Mom is happy there and already friendly with the other residents. She and Clara, one of her housemates, joke about how much they'd liked playing jacks when they were schoolgirls and would like to try it again. But Clara figures she couldn't get down on the floor, and Mom figures she couldn't get back up again. So they've settled for just reminiscing about it.

Meanwhile, Howard and I spent a delightful week in Jacksonville, Florida, with our new grandson, Savino Meyer Tessler, and his parents, Steve and Beth, who are stationed with the Navy there.

We arrived in Phoenix the first of April and stayed through May. With plans for a trip to Alaska sometime next year, one of the things we did during our stay was to buy an additional fifth-wheel travel trailer. This one is a twenty-foot Front Range, which you've probably never heard of; I think we have the only one in captivity.

If it doesn't fall apart, maybe we'll have a collector's item someday. It's clean and cozy and fits our budget. Until we're ready for our trip, it will remain in storage in Phoenix.

ON THE ROAD—June 16-25, 1996

After spending the first two weeks of June in Albuquerque, our next destination was Springfield, Missouri, where we visited my Thomas cousins at Ann's house. She knew of a great all-you-can-eat pizza place, and after three platefuls apiece, we waddled back to Ann's to visit some more.

Ann added an interesting piece to the mystery of our great-grandfather, James Gibson. We already knew that at the beginning of the Civil War, he joined forces with the Union Army, although the rest of his family, all from North Carolina, were strong supporters of the Confederacy. His brother Hardy was killed during "Pickett's Charge" at Gettysburg, and—as we'd learned recently—their own father (our great-great-grandfather Martin Gibson) had joined the Confederate army briefly.

Much of our family history is lost because of the split in loyalties. I'm sad to say our great-grandfather seemed to be the one unwilling to make peace. Ann learned he never reconciled with his daughter because she'd married a Confederate officer. I don't know what he expected; after all, she had always lived in the South. What sad things war does to people.

MICHIGAN—June 25 through July 28, 1996

From Springfield, we drove across Illinois and Indiana, stopping here and there, and finally arrived at a campground near East Lansing the 25th. We parked by a lake with a lot of frogs, which we heard begging for bud-weis-er every night. There were also lots of big mosquitoes—sometimes it was hard to distinguish them from airplanes. But we couldn't complain about the scenery. Grass! Trees!

We saw an MSU production of *The Rainmaker*. Sharon said she'd heard that the play might not make sense to folks up here where it rains a lot, but anyone from the southwest would tune right in.

We spent a day in Holland, Michigan, where we visited Windmill Island. Although we had missed the peak season in the spring, the island was still filled with lovely tulips of every color. We also toured a windmill there and watched Da Klompers klomping/dancing in their wooden sabots.

Across the state, we've seen motel signs that advertise "clean rooms." These are usually modest places across the street from the luxury hotels that advertise beachfront views. Let's see—is it an "either-or" proposition? ("We have expensive rooms with nice views but can't be bothered with cleaning" or "clean windowless rooms.") Those, along with places that sell "diesel ice cream," give us something to mull over.

We eventually arrived in the upper peninsula of Michigan ("da U.P."), mispronouncing names right and left. Our first stop was at the Michihistrigan Campground in the town of Gould. While in the area, we enjoyed a pleasant hike around Seney Wildlife Refuge. Here's a list of the wildlife we saw: *Many* Canada geese, several mosquitoes, some ducks, a few swans, a few shiny-backed turtles, one loon, one bald eagle, one frog, and one wild iris.

Next we parked at the Wandering Wheels Campground in Munising. We spent one day visiting the nearby Pictured Rocks National Lakeshore. The weather was perfect, the sky "New-Mexico blue," and Lake Superior an even deeper blue.

However, the most fun part of our day was spent in a dark, unscenic, unclassy bar.

First, you need to understand that the only thing that seems to connect (1) Upper Michigan and (2) Lower Michigan is the Mackinac *Bridge*. They are almost like two separate countries. We heard that "the yoopers" ("da yoopers") have their own unique culture and dialect. Maybe it's because the land is so rugged that the people seem so ruggedly independent, eh?

Also, we have to explain about "pasties" (rhymes with "past," not "paste"), which are like stuffed sopaipillas, except the crust is more like a flaky pie crust, and the basic filling is, or used to be, beef and potatoes. They were originally the mainstay of the Cornish miners. Nowadays you can get "vegetarian pasties" to satisfy the health nuts, but that's neither here nor there. They say you can't get authentic pasties anywhere but "da U.P."

Before coming to Munising, we had stopped at a rather dingy bar and tried some pasties for the first time. They were surprisingly fresh and tasty, so we wanted to try again. I didn't want to eat at a "quick stop" place, however, because I figured they'd probably be microwaved instead of freshly made.

So we saw a restaurant/bar, Sylvester's, in Munising, that advertised hot pasties, and thought it looked like a good bet. It turned out that the restaurant part wasn't even open, but that was OK; we could still order pasties, which the bartender was happy to microwave.

The only customers besides us were another couple and two bikers. The other couple, Mike and Jeannie, had ordered pasties as well, but evidently the bartender (Sam) didn't nuke Mike's enough, and it was still cold. So Mike went up to the bar and asked, very quietly, "Are these supposed to be frozen?"

Sam was apologetic, and immediately re-nuked Mike's order. However, since the whole place was so unbusy, everyone there knew what had happened, and the bikers started ribbing Sam. Jeannie said it was the first time they'd ever had pasties, so they didn't know what to expect—thought maybe they were *supposed* to be frozen. Then the bikers kidded Sam even more, and we were all (including Sam) laughing and joking about it.

I asked Jeannie where they were from (since they obviously weren't yoopers either). She said they lived near Detroit. Then it was Sam's turn to kid them. "Oh," he said, "You live 'below the bridge.' You're trolls!"

Soon the seven of us were having a blast, chatting away like old friends. Seems odd that a simple mistake could turn the afternoon into a party.

If you ever come to Michigan, "downstate" (where the trolls live) is where we found some of the prettiest and most picturesque Victorian neighborhoods we've yet to see. Especially in Romeo, Petoskey, and Bay View.

We discovered that Romeo had been a link on the Underground Railroad during the Civil War. We drove over to see the Octagon House, one of the underground "stations" along the way. Although the house—so named because of its unusual shape—was closed, simply walking around the grounds struck us with the reality of things we'd only read about in history books.

One of the things you might want to skip is a "wet burrito." This must be a "troll" concoction, and the one I tried consisted of stiff canned beans and wilted lettuce, wrapped in a preservative-laden tortilla, and covered with something tan and gravyish.

Something in the U.P. we should have skipped: We took a buggy (as in insecty) hike to an abandoned lighthouse. We'd applied ourselves liberally with mosquito repellent; ironically, there were NO—as in "zero"—mosquitoes, but the stable flies *loved* the "repellent."

We did skip Horseshoe Falls, near Munising, which turned out to be a tourist trap. There was only one entrance to the trail to the falls, through a tacky souvenir shop, with a $2.00 charge. The fee itself wasn't unreasonable, but to us it was obscene to charge anything to look at a waterfall. Sort of like charging to look at a sunset. Instead we took a short (free) hike to beautiful Munising Falls.

We found the greatest used-book store, 84 Charing Cross, Eh?, in Munising. It was large, well organized, and contained almost every book imaginable. I found a copy of Great-Great-Uncle Will Stoddard's book, *Two Arrows*, which I bought for $7.00. As might be expected (since it was published over 100 years ago), much of the story (and the style) is outdated, but I admired his theme of bringing harmony between the "red" and "white" races.

Next on our route, we discovered the wonderful town of Ontonagon. Small (one traffic light), quaint, untouristy. Friendly ladies running the RV park. One said she'd been asked how they could stand living in such an isolated community (120 miles from a TV station; 50 miles from a WalMart) and the *cold* winters.

She said, well, they didn't have tornadoes, hurricanes, earthquakes, floods, etc. And they *do* have plenty of firewood. She said they have visitors all winter who come up to cross-country ski, go snowmobiling, etc. One guy even stayed in a tent for a few days in 10° weather, building a campfire in the evening, and curling up in a down sleeping bag at night. I shiver to think of it. These yoopers are a hardy lot, eh?

During our stay there, we also visited Hancock and Houghton, twin cities in the northernmost part of Michigan. In Houghton we discovered a Mexican restaurant called Los Dos Amigos. We didn't eat there, but read the menu on the window. Next to the menu was a whole page of funny explanations. I especially liked the first one:

> "Who said anything about 'authentic' Mexican food? Hey!
> Where do you think you are? This is the U.P."

Hancock was settled by Finnish people. The street signs are written in both Finnish and English, and both Finnish flags (featuring a blue cross on a white background) and American flags fly all along Main Street (Valtakatu). We enjoyed soaking in a culture that was unfamiliar to us.

WISCONSIN—July 29 through August 9, 1996

After spending five weeks in Michigan, we decided it was time to move on. Our first stop was in Eagle River, Wisconsin. There we were happy to learn that Elliana Patricia Michelle Moran was born to Mike and Norma on July 29.

We spent three gray, *chilly* days there. One day the high reached 58°, which was 22° below normal, the weatherman said. Better than 22° above, said he. We watched lots of videos.

We arrived in Rhinelander August 1, and enjoyed nice weather from then on. As usual, the lone pay phone was constantly in use—there was always a line. The second night we got to chatting with the lady sitting on the "waiting bench" with us, and when we told her we were calling Sharon to wish her happy birthday, she said, "Would you like all of us to sing to her?"

So she collected her teen-age kids and their friends who were hanging around waiting their turn at the phone, plus a few friendly passersby, and by the time Howard and I made our call, there was quite a "choir"! I think the choir got as big a kick out of it as Sharon did.

As you can see, this was a friendly park, and I soon discovered the town was just as friendly. I had been browsing in a gift shop for a few minutes when the owner said, "I know this sounds odd, but are you going to be here awhile?" I said yes, and she said she had to run next door for just a minute to pick up a fax—if I didn't mind being left alone.

I was mildly flabbergasted. I certainly didn't mind, and she was hardly gone two minutes (and I wound up buying some stuff). But she had lots of *expensive* items in her shop, and I marveled that she'd leave it in the hands of a stranger. I tried to picture this happening in Phoenix or Albuquerque.

IOWA—August 10-13, 1996

We spent a few days in Iowa, which—up till now—we'd thought of simply as someplace we had to go through to get from Point A to Point B. But we soon realized we'd underestimated this interesting and multi-cultural state.

And we can't say our time there was uneventful. Our next-door neighbors, Rookie, and his girlfriend, Goofy, arrived at our RV park one afternoon in their brand-new motorhome. Their "teamwork" was, to be charitable, a little iffy.

Goofy: (Giggle, giggle) I guess this is where we park. (Giggle) Shall we park on the grass? (Giggle, giggle)

At this point, nosy neighbor (i.e., yo) goes to the window to observe. I'm relieved to see that Rookie is ignoring the grass and backing onto the pad, or in its general direction. Goofy is standing off to the side near Rookie, counting butterflies as best I can tell. Neither of them has any idea what's happening behind them.

Noise: CLUNK, CLUNK, CLUNK
Rookie: What was that?
Goofy: (Giggle, giggle) I don't know. (Giggle, giggle, giggle)
Rookie: (Still backing up) Did I hit something?
Goofy: (Giggle, giggle, giggle) Yes, you ran over the picnic table! (This is followed by riotous laughter.)

Rookie stops, goes forward a few feet. Another neighbor comes over and rescues the picnic table. Now Goofy goes over and stands next to Rookie's door, where she has even less visibility than before. Rookie starts backing again.

Rookie: Should I go back further?
Goofy: (Giggle, giggle) It's up to you. (Giggle, giggle)

To our collective relief, he finally got situated without demolishing the whole park.

ON THE ROAD—August and September, 1996

I wish I could describe to you the gorgeous fields of huge sunflowers we saw as we crossed Kansas on our way to Colorado. Sometimes it looked like a bright gold carpet spread out between fields of corn. I guess the sunflowers are grown commercially there— we'd never seen so many in one place before, and they were in such neat, compact rows, they had to have been planted. Except for that, nothing too exciting to report from Kansas—no tornadoes, no lions, cowardly or otherwise.

Howard called ahead to a park near Albuquerque that some friends had recommended. He was told the park had VERY STRICT RULES (the lady talked in capital letters and underlining) and we'd have to send in an *application* so they could decide if we were worthy of staying there.

Not long afterward we got the application plus a lengthy and ungrammatical set of rules in the mail. Most of the rules actually seemed pretty reasonable. The only one I'm not sure I can live with: "Do not park or drive onto the landscaping." This was quite a disappointment, since running over flowers is my favorite thing.

Don't breathe a word of this, or we might lose out, because one of the rules was not to gossip or complain about the management.

"WE ARE WATCHING."

HERE AND THERE—
October through December 1996

Since we had stored our Front Range trailer in Phoenix, we were now faced with the prospect of shuffling two RVs down to Zapata for the winter. So we bounced from Albuquerque to Zapata, where we parked the Alpenlite, then drove to Phoenix trailerless to pick up the Front Range. We brought it back to Zapata, parked it in a storage area at our RV park, and finally got settled in before the year was out. During all this maneuvering, we visited family and friends along the way.

For one reason or another, the Behms were late getting their Christmas tree this year, and pickin's were slim by the time they found one. Our son-in-law Michael was feeling pretty discouraged as he hauled their "Charlie-Brown" selection into the house. But four-year-old Aubrey, bless her heart, said, "Oh, Daddy, that is *the most beautiful* tree I've ever seen!"

A happy way to end the year.

1997

ZAPATA, TEXAS
January 1 through April 4, 1997

January wasn't a very good month for us. One or the other of us was under the weather throughout the month—and the weather was yukky to be under: mostly cold and gloomy. And we both took falls—Howard slipped on the icy steps, and I tripped because I wasn't looking where I was going. Nothing serious, just something to add to our list of frustrations.

Now that that's out of the way, we can tell you about the silver linings. As always, we delight in the fragrance of the Rapps' lemon trees near our home, as well as the taste of the sweet ruby grapefruit Dean Flowers shares with us from her trees.

One January day, a group of us visited "Santa's Texas Workshop," which is open from September through March. This is the home of the three Minten sisters, retired schoolteachers who live in the small community of La Gloria (near the small town of Falfurrias). Every year they select a new decorating theme for Christmas. And for them, Christmas lasts all year long. Above all, their wish is to keep the true spirit of Christmas alive by sharing their home and combining the fun and the reverence of the season. Not only are visitors treated to rooms filled with lavish decorations, but the sisters also provide music, entertaining stories, and tasty refreshments.

Howard's been doing lots of little fixit jobs on the Front Range, and we've been poring over info about Alaska. Although our ferry trip through the Inside Passage won't begin till the first of June, we made reservations several months in advance. Once that commitment was made, it began to seem real.

March 1, 1997

Suddenly it's summer—got up to 98° today. We had one day of spring—that was yesterday. Our friends the Garzas barbecued chicken here for about thirty people, so we were glad our one spring day was so cooperative, and the party fun.

Howard and I also had fun celebrating my birthday in the Brownsville/South Padre Island area. When we arrived at South Padre, it was raining and the city park was full. So we went back to a little town twenty miles away, Los Fresnos, and made some happy discoveries. Not only did we like the RV park and town itself, but we found a wonderful restaurant there called Julia's. So our bad luck quickly turned into good.

Another convenient thing: We were only a few miles from Brownsville, where I'd wanted to do some family-tree searches. I knew that my great-grandfather James Gibson was stationed at Ft. Brown after the Civil War. The Union Army was there to keep the "troublemaking Texans" in line, I suppose.

At the library, I found the records I was looking for on microfilm. I also found some fascinating statistics on the census pages. Most of the soldiers living in his barracks were foreign-born. On James G.'s page, I counted only twelve out of forty born in the US. (He, of course, was the only southerner.) There were six from New York, fourteen from Ireland, seven from Prussia, the rest from a variety of states and countries.

One of the census items to be filled out—that none of them had checked, I'm happy to say—was "whether deaf and dumb, blind, insane, or idiotic."

Back to the present tense: We drove over to South Padre, but the weather was still so temperamental, we decided to skip beach walks and go to our favorite restaurant, Blackbeard's, instead. It used to be kind of low-key and rustic. But it's become quite popular since we were there ten years ago and is now more upscale and pricy. Food's still good though.

FROM TEXAS TO ARIZONA—April 5-12, 1997

Nothing like pulling out of the driveway on the way out of town to make you suddenly appreciate the people and places you're leaving behind. In our eagerness to get on the road, I don't think we realized how much we would miss our extended Zapata family . . . .

We even viewed the road to Laredo with new eyes—everything bright and green after our spring rains. The bluebonnets got thicker as we neared Johnson City, and we took the recommended Willow City tour. This made me think of Wyoming, where people putter through the Grand Tetons and Yellowstone, jumping out of their cars "wherever" and "whenever" to take pictures of moose and buffalo. Here in the hill country, folks stop to take pictures of bluebonnets (with themselves sitting among them).

It was nice that no one was in a hurry—and of course we got a picture of ourselves in the midst of the flowers too. We found the white Texas poppies as gorgeous as the bluebonnets. So, if we don't get beaucoup pictures of all those enormous fish Howard will be catching in Alaska, we'll just have to circulate photos of ourselves as "flower children."

At the RV park we chatted with a couple who said, "Would you believe, we came down from *Kansas* just to see the bluebonnets?" Yes, we would!

We also stopped in Luckenbach. Didn't see Waylon and Willie and the boys, but laughed at a sign over the bar that read, "If you need credit, you don't need a beer."

PHOENIX, ARIZONA—April 13-23, 1997

We enjoyed our stay in Phoenix, once we got off the interstate. We keep forgetting that Phoenix is a tangle of multi-laned highways crammed with impatient people changing the aforementioned lanes as frequently as possible—all outracing one another in an effort to be "first" to wherever they're going (in a thousand different directions, of course).

Once we got on the residential streets, where traffic slowed down to a mere 60 mph, we could enjoy, as always, the bougainvillea, palo verde, jacaranda, and bird of paradise in full bloom.

Margot is twelve now; Adrienne, eleven. At their respective schools, Margot is learning to play the violin; Adrienne, the flute. They treated us to a duet of the songs they've learned so far. They're not quite ready for the Boston Pops, but to our ears, it was a sweet sweet sound.

ALBUQUERQUE, NEW MEXICO
April 25 through May 6, 1997

April 28, 1997

What a surprise to find that Tucumcari, New Mexico, made the Weather Channel headlines the other day! A spring storm had dumped ten inches of snow on the town. Didn't catch any mention of what the storm was doing in Albuquerque; i.e., closing off the interstates in three directions! We found that out from the truckers on their CBs as we traveled from Winslow into town.

Guess we were lucky there were no problems on the west side of town, and we were able to arrive at our RV park without any problem. I think whoever built this park decided to cram as many spaces together as possible to accommodate all the people who were willing to be uncomfortable for a few days to watch the balloons (and pay $$$ for the privilege).

Of course it isn't "balloon season," but we do have a view of the mountains and are snug (very snug), safe, and more-or-less sound.

You might remember how I've mispronounced names all across the North American continent. Well, getting back to the Weather

Channel, the aforementioned (don't you love that word?) spring storm had also wreaked havoc in several Texas locations, including Deaf Smith County. The weather person, obviously not a Texan, had pronounced it "Deaf Smith" County.

Now it was *my* turn to act superior and shout, "DEEF Smith, you dingaling, DEEF Smith!"

ON THE ROAD—May 7-20, 1997

As always, we had fun reading signs posted here and there. At one intersection in Phoenix, we found an interesting conglomeration tacked up on a utility pole. Under the one about "Fast Divorce" was another about dental hygiene, then another about carpet cleaning.

We wondered if you could get your divorce *and* have your teeth and carpet cleaned—all done at the same time and place for one low price. Howard says that pretty soon folks can step up to their ATM machine and get cash and a divorce all in one fell swoop.

In Albuquerque, we saw a sign advertising a "Huge Adult Video Arcade." I thought that meant you could watch videos featuring overweight adults, while Howard thought it meant only overweight adults could patronize the arcade. Our difference in interpretation, he explained, only goes to show that men and women are from different planets.

Not far from there was a place featuring "nude demonstrations." Again we had varying ideas on exactly what was meant. Were unclothed salespeople demonstrating used cars? Tupperware, perhaps?

Ah well, as you can see, traveling gives one a vast opportunity to ponder life's mysteries.

Our first night after leaving Albuquerque, we stayed at one of those campgrounds where they park RVs two to a space. So the nice lady gave us site #6 and told us to pull forward as far as possible, to leave room in case someone pulled into #5 behind us.

There was not another soul in the park at all.

Howard said, "I bet before the night's over, there'll be two or three more RVs pulling in."

I said, "Oh, I'm sure there'll be more than that. I bet at least six."

We were both wrong. *Nobody* else pulled in. At all. So, for the very *first* time in our RVing history, we were the *first* (if only) ones to leave the next morning.

BRITISH COLUMBIA—May 21-22, 1997

Our crossing into Canada—at Osoyous, BC, just north of the Washington border—was "interesting." First, the young woman at the customs/inspection station asked what state or province we were from. Texas, we told her. Then she asked a number of other questions. Did we have any liquor?

Howard:	No.
Customs Person:	None at all?
Howard:	No.
CP:	No wine coolers? Not even a beer?
Howard:	No, we don't indulge.

(Which was true for the time being. Not that it would have mattered, since it isn't illegal to possess a specified amount of liquor.)

Moving right along: Next she wanted to know about firearms. No firearms, Howard told her.

"You don't carry a handgun when you travel?" she asked, sounding incredulous.

"No," Howard answered.

She was surprised because, she told us, she always had to be careful when TEXANS came through. (We hard-drinkin' Texans do love our guns!) She was very pleasant about it all, and evidently believed us since, after a couple more questions about our criminal records or lack thereof, she let us continue on.

We suspected she might have seen too many John Wayne movies, but on the off-chance she might have seen some Al Capone movies too, Howard said later it was probably just as well he didn't mention he was originally from Chicago.

Our next adventure occurred at noon. We'd chosen a "dotted" route from our roadmap, and stopped for lunch at a roadside picnic table. We ate inside our RV, and afterwards, as we were coming out, Howard stopped me in my tracks. He pointed to a large black bear just yards away, apparently searching for garbage left by careless picnickers.

I *know* (from all the visits to National Parks where you're *expected* to see bears, only I never do) that you're not supposed to look bears in the eye. I wonder if the bears have a similar rule in their manual regarding human beings?

But the bear and I stared at each other as if hypnotized. He finally turned and lumbered off into the nearby bushes, but didn't really leave the area. We hotfooted it to the truck and drove away before he could reappear.

The next-best exciting thing was discovering a pileated woodpecker in our RV park the next night. OK, OK, so that's not exactly in the same heart-stopping category as a bear encounter. But to us bird-watchers, it was quite a treat. These woodpeckers usually avoid populated areas and are difficult to find, especially "up close and personal." This one, however, was completely oblivious to everything around it, and we could practically reach out and touch it.

PRINCE GEORGE, BRITISH COLUMBIA
May 23-25, 1997

People have been remarkably friendly wherever we've stayed. After lunch one afternoon, Howard asked the KFC lady where we could find a grocery store.

She told us what sounded like, "There's an Overweighty's just around the corner."

We wondered if that's where she thought folks like us (who sport a few extra pounds) ought to be shopping. Turned out the store was named "Overwaitea's."

Shopping in Canada is fun. All the labels are written in both French and English, including Old El Paso Tortilla Chips (les croustilles de tortilla au maïs blanc de style restaurant).

I needed Coffeemate, which in the States is called a "non-dairy creamer"—a contradiction in terms, I must admit. But in Canada it's called a "coffee *whitener*," which doesn't sound very appetizing to me—more like the stuff we once used to white out typing mistakes. The French is less jarring: "colorant à café.

Anyway, when I got back home I compared the ingredients listed on the labels. They don't sound very appetizing either. Just what *is* dipotassium phosphate?

One day we wandered down to the town park and lucked into a Heritage Fair celebrating the various cultures in Canada. The park was filled with families taking in the pleasant surroundings. We saw several kids getting their faces painted, others following a clown on stilts. We especially enjoyed a performance by a group of young girls dressed in colorful Scottish costumes as they performed Highland dances.

The park is enormous, with lots of trees and grass. I guess this is the way parks are supposed to be, but I always get carried away by greenery.

They call it "Beautiful British Columbia"—and we've yet to see anything ugly.

PRINCE RUPERT, BRITISH COLUMBIA
May 30-June 3, 1997

Looking at a map of British Columbia, you can see that the populated area lies along the southern region. And the route between Prince George and Prince Rupert, in the middle of the province, looks like 450 miles of desolation.

But once again we found that the journey itself took many fascinating turns. If we hadn't been on a schedule, I think we could have spent the rest of the summer in Smithers, a small Alpine-type village surrounded by steep snow-covered mountains. A ski resort in winter, and a favorite of golfers in warmer weather.

Prince Rupert, another charming town, was our last stop before ferrying to Alaska. On our last day there, someone told us that the best place to watch bald eagles was at a landfill. So, odd as it might seem, one of the highlights of our trip was visiting Prince Rupert's City Dump!

We were astounded at the number of bald eagles we saw there—more than the combined total we saw anywhere else. One of the things that fascinated me was discovering the sound these eagles make—sort of a quavery, tremulous cry—not what I'd have expected from such powerful majestic birds.

KETCHIKAN, ALASKA—June 4-6, 1997

According to Charles Kuralt in his book *America*, saying that Ketchikan is rainy is like saying that San Francisco is hilly.

We arrived raincoated, having been forewarned that Ketchikan, Alaska, is THE rainiest place in North America, with an average yearly rainfall of 172 inches (give or take a drop).

So what attracted us to this moist town that would, in all probability, drizzle all over our newly bought raingear? And why did we, like Charles Kuralt, add it to our list of favorites?

Calling Ketchikan scenic is not only an understatement, but this description fits all of the Inside Passage of Alaska as well. The waterway that zigzags a thousand miles from Ketchikan to Skagway, dodging thousands of islands, flows along a wide canyon, with snow-capped mountains rising suddenly and steeply on one or both sides, or—where the channel curves—on all sides.

This said, I must confess: Our *introduction* to Ketchikan was not too entrancing. When we arrived from Prince Rupert on the Malaspina, it was 2:45 in the wee hours of an early June morning. Because this was *southern* Alaska, the famed midnight sun was not shining. So we drove fourteen miles in rain and pitch-blackness to our RV Park. (Eighteen miles if you count missing the turn-off and making a U-turn.)

Not wanting to rouse the whole neighborhood with the noisy task of see-sawing, cranking, and unhitching, we pulled into the first available slot, tossed our bedrolls onto our bed, and slept away what was left of the night.

When daylight broke, with its typical hum of campground activity, we tracked down our pre-assigned site. It turned out there was no way we could ever have pulled into it, even in the light of day, much less in the dark of night. It was simply too short.

Since this was the third time in a row we'd been "short-sited," the reason finally dawned on us: Small campers vastly outnumber all other kinds of RVs we've seen in this region. Our various campground hosts were merely unaccustomed to parking such "massive" rigs as ours.

This was funny to us, since our 20-foot Front Range was the shortest trailer we could find, and we'd bought it specifically for our Alaska trip. Problem was, our hosts hadn't counted on the *combined* length of truck and trailer, and they would try to squeeze our entire rig into a twenty-foot space. However they were unfailingly cheerful and accommodating about helping us relocate each time.

Once we had rearranged ourselves at this latest park, we settled down to breakfast. Imagine our surprise when we discovered the local water was only a few shades lighter than the coffee we intended to brew. We were assured that the color came from the tannin in the muskeg/ground cover. Not only that, the water was said to be the purest we would find anywhere.

We dared to test it after boiling it for the coffee. But since the coffee tasted so good, we decided to close our eyes and drink the water ice-cold and undiluted. Imagine our further surprise to find it as pure as promised.

We hardly batted an eye at our tan showers. And by the time we'd gotten dressed and "suited out"—Howard in his olive-drab raincoat from Cabella's, and I in my $4.98 turquoise poncho from WalMart—we were ready to discover the "real" Ketchikan.

Our first impression of Ketchikan by daylight was of picturesque houses splashed against the base of Deer Mountain like colorful swirls of icing on a three-tiered birthday cake. The mountain ranges continue rising, almost vertically, effectively defining the eastern boundary of town. Above the houses, the mountainside is lush and green.

A narrow five-mile stretch of the business area of town (including schools, churches, and museums) slices between the Tongass channel on one side and the houses on the other. Narrow = about four blocks.

But beyond the scenery, Ketchikan has a swaggering charm—a vitality—that's hard to pin down. Despite the throngs of tourists spilling out of the cruise ships, and the shops where only tourists shop, it has a small-town neighborliness that invites those of us from "The Outside" to join in and weather the weather.

Only someone hardy enough to survive its harsh winters would choose to live in Alaska. Ketchikan residents are no exception. Like most Alaskans, they are tough and unpretentious. No one cares whether your outfit comes from L.L. Bean or the Salvation Army thrift store. At the same time, Ketchikansans are warm and friendly, happy to share their town and its treasures.

We found the Tongass Historical Museum an excellent place to stop and chat with an eclectic mix of residents, including Haida weavers and Tlingit artisans.

At the Saxman Native Village, the Totem Heritage Center, and Totem Bight State Park, people explained the symbolism of various totem figures and told some of the underlying—often humorous—stories surrounding them.

At Saxman there's a totem depicting a short-legged Abraham Lincoln. It's actually intended to represent the USS Lincoln, the Navy vessel that created quite a stir when it docked in the area.

There's another totem dedicated to, but not honoring, former Secretary of State William Seward. Poor Mr. Seward. Folks back home sneered at or railed against his "folly" in purchasing "that worthless wasteland known as Alaska."

He didn't fare too much better among the Tlingit Natives during his Alaskan visits. They gave him a series of "potlatches," elaborate feasts demonstrating the wealth and generosity of the hosts. However, tribal culture dictates that the recipients respond with similar or even more lavish celebrations later on.

Mr. Seward, who didn't know anything about the nature of potlatches, and didn't have a Visitor Center to explain it all, failed to reciprocate.

As a result, perched atop a totem pole in Saxman is an abstract figure representing the clueless Mr. Seward, wearing nothing but a hat encircled with five rings, denoting the five potlatches he owes.

When the storytelling ended, clusters of blue and white striped umbrellas bobbed rhythmically toward the Gray Line buses, while we turned toward town. There we had lunch at a cozy coffee shop, built—like virtually all of the waterfront structures—on pilings over the harbor.

During our stay in Ketchikan we window-shopped at T-shirt/ trinket shops, at elegant jewelry stores, and at everything in between.

And what about that summertime rain? It's a come-and-go, off-and-on-again kind of rain. Soft and gentle when it's on. Wait five minutes and it's off. After a while you hardly notice, hardly bother with your pristine raingear. After a while, like the residents, you wink and say with a smile, "What rain?"

"OUR FERRY FRIENDS"—June 8, 1997

It was raining in Petersburg and continued to rain all day off and on, mostly on. Not many people got off the Malaspina when we docked at 4:30 a.m. Since ours was only a day trip, we parked at the ferry terminal, ate breakfast, then walked into town.

Petersburg was originally a Norwegian fishing village. It is tiny and definitely untouristy, the channel being too narrow to allow cruise ships. Because it was Sunday, there was little activity.

Walking by the Lutheran Church, we could hear the congregation singing "Ode to Joy." The sound of their voices permeating the neighborhood was truly joyful. Other than that, we'd begun to think we wouldn't have missed much if we'd skipped Petersburg.

After we returned to our Front Range and had lunch, we noticed other RVs drifting into the terminal, so we took our place in line. This marked a turning point in our day.

The Alaska Marine Highway asks that RVs arrive at least two hours before departure (three hours in Prince Rupert, since we'd had to go through customs). Something we'd discovered from the beginning is a camaraderie that quickly develops among wait-in-liners.

So during the intervals when the rain in Petersburg reduced itself to mere drizzles, everyone circulated around the parking lot, striking up conversations with one another.

Then in the midst of all our getting acquainted came the news: Our ferry, the Columbia, due to dock at 4:40 that afternoon, had developed engine trouble and returned to Wrangell for repairs. There would be "an hour's delay." Every hour stretched into another gray rainy hour.

We eventually gravitated toward the waiting room in the terminal, where everyone's grumbling soon gave way to a sense of fun. Someone sent out for pizza. Howard and I joined our new-acquaintances-soon-to-be-friends in a game of Chinese dominoes. Another table of six was within yelling distance, with hilarious competition quickly underway. The person with the liveliest sense of humor was Dave Damon. He was burly and bearded with dark curly hair, sparkling hazel eyes, and strong opinions.

The lone agent manning the terminal kept periodic contact with the ailing ferry, and after one of his calls, came over to our tables with a big grin. "My boss wanted to know what was going on here. He said that judging from the background noise, he wondered if he'd been patched to Reno by mistake."

Shortly after that, a fire engine shrieked by, momentarily silencing our rowdiness. Then Dave spoke up. "The sun must have come out!" he shouted gleefully. "And they hadn't seen it in so long, they thought something was on fire!"

By the time the Columbia arrived at 11:30 that night (and finally departed about 1:00 a.m.), we had not only turned a glum and frustrating situation into a party, but had also connected with folks we would continue to meet throughout our journey along the Inside Passage.

I hate to think what we would have missed if we had skipped this stop, or if the ferry had been on time.

SITKA, ALASKA—"THE PARIS OF THE PACIFIC" June 9-12, 1997

If Ketchikan's lusty past brings to mind rowdy fishermen and painted ladies, Sitka's illustrious past recalls scholarly clerics and Russian princesses.

It was the Russian aspect of Alaska's history that I found so intriguing. One of the first things I learned, the term "America" in conjunction with "Russian America" and its settlements meant "NORTH America," and had nothing to do with the United States.

The Russians who colonized Sitka designated it capital of Russian America. They called it "New Archangel," and the golden domes of the Orthodox Cathedral of St. Michael the Archangel still grace the city.

There are no leftover Russians in Sitka, however, except for Native Alaskans of mixed ancestry. The original Russian residents, mostly government officials and their families, were swiftly banished when the US bought Alaska and installed its own territorial government.

One sad result was that Princess Maksoutov took her own life within the year, heartbroken over being exiled from the home she loved.

The US returned the town's name to an adaptation of its original Tlingit one (Shee-Atika), and established Sitka as the new territorial Capital of Alaska. On the grounds of the old Baranof castle, the site where the transfer of ownership was completed, are markers commemorating Alaska's "new birthday"—October 18, 1867. Today Sitkans celebrate this event with even more fanfare than the Fourth of July.

Our stay in Sitka started typically enough: That is to say, it was raining when we de-ferried and caravanned with our new-found friends to a nearby RV park. The next day dawned bright and sunny, and we all tumbled out of our RVs like clowns out of toy cars, converging in the center of the campground, coffee mugs in hand.

One of the couples we liked was camped in nearby Starrigavan National Park, while another was staying at the Sitka Hotel downtown. Otherwise, the "domino crowd" was intact. This gave us a chance to get better acquainted with Connie and Wayne Butaud, fellow Texans.

We were all in high spirits, warmed by the sun and invigorated by a sense of adventure. After all, here we were in Sitka, the Paris of the Pacific, the jewel of Russian America. And of all the wonderful places we visited in Alaska, Connie and I later agreed that this city became our favorite.

The seven-mile drive into town was a pleasure in itself. Halibut Point Road skirted Sitka Sound, and the view was breathtaking. Even the grocery store was situated on a scenic point, with a magnificent view of Mt. Edgecumbe volcano and other snow-capped mountains across the sound.

The residents were relishing the 70° "heat wave," and we took advantage of the balmy day to take a narrated bus tour around town. Our driver, Kelly, was enthusiastic about both the weather and the city.

We drove out to "Old Sitka," which happened to be around the corner from the ferry terminal. There we were reminded that history is never one-dimensional. Just as there is a more dignified side to Ketchikan's past, there is a less noble side to Sitka's. And Sitka's history, in all its many facets, is intertwined with the mystique of the present-day town.

The first Russian-American venture into Sitka proved disastrous. The resident Kiksadi Tlingits were not too enthralled with the Russians' plan to enslave them, and tensions increased over the next few years until finally the Tlingits destroyed the Russian colony. Old Sitka marks the site of the massacre.

When the Russian-American Company, under the leadership of Governor Alexander Baranof, returned a few years later (1804), they chose a different site (where the Sitka National Park stands now) and defeated the Tlingits. Although there were no further uprisings on the part of the Tlingits—or attempts at slavery on the part of the Russians—a climate of trust never quite developed between the two.

Kelly also pointed out Governor Baranof's legacy, an area known today as Castle Hill, around which the Russians had once built a wall to restrict access by the Tlingits. Today both castle and wall are gone, but the grounds are a historical landmark, and an impressive view of the city can be seen from the hill.

On a more mundane note, someone asked Kelly how much she paid for groceries. "Well," she answered, "when the ferry brings supplies as scheduled, I pay $3.00 for a half-gallon of milk. When the ferry can't get through and we have everything *flown* in, I pay $5.00 instead."

We learned much of the local history and folklore while visiting the Sitka National Historical Park. One legend that particularly fascinated me was about a young man who'd become so evil the only solution anyone could find was to have him executed and burned. However, as he was being cremated, his ashes rose from the fire and turned into mosquitoes, and that's why we're tormented with mosquitoes today. Best explanation I've heard so far.

The next day we visited the Russian Bishop's House, which is also maintained by the National Park Service. When the Russian Orthodox Church established a mission in 1840, Bishop Ivan Veniaminov did much toward promoting harmony, simply by his innate kindness and desire to befriend the Natives. He translated the Bible into Tlingit and Aleut dialects and educated Native children in the three Rs as well as the Orthodox faith.

St. Michael's Orthodox Church was built in 1840 by Finnish Lutheran carpenters who quickly organized their own congregation. Their present structure, across the street from the Orthodox Church, is very modest by comparison. (Some say the plainness was decreed by the Russians.)

In any event, visitors are invited to tour the Lutheran Church, which sounded interesting to us. Unfortunately, the guide-du-jour hadn't done her homework. Not long into her spiel, she made the startling announcement that theirs was the very first church established on the Pacific coast of North America.

"Really!" I exclaimed, feeling my eyes pop open and question marks sprout out of my head like those of a cartoon character.

"Yes, we were the first."

"Even before those in California?" I kept probing, as I mentally reviewed coastal missions dating back to the 1500s.

"Yes, we were the first," she insisted, her needle obviously stuck in its groove.

We quickly lost interest in anything else she had to say, thanked her, and fled.

Other religions have made their mark in Sitka too. The Presbyterians established Sheldon Jackson College, whose museum features one of Alaska's finest exhibits of Native history and culture.

St. Peter's-by-the-Sea Episcopal Church also welcomes visitors. Its simple but striking log structure overlooks the harbor and is as appealing and beautiful in its own way as St. Michael's.

When it came time to leave Sitka, we optimistically lined up at 3:00 p.m. per schedule. However, we were warned that the ferry's departure time was always a little iffy, due to the tides. In the meantime, we got to experience another kind of warning: the ear-piercing tsunami emergency test sirens at the terminal! The Matanuska finally departed seven hours later.

JUNEAU, ALASKA—June 14-19, 1997

Monday was cheerful and sunny—"hot" by Juneau standards (70°), but brisk and cool to us. Since we could buy an all-day fare, we took the trolley off and on, first visiting St. Nicholas Russian Orthodox Church and its next-door neighbor, "the world's smallest Roman Catholic Cathedral."

We re-boarded the trolley, getting off at the State Capitol where we took a guided tour with Dave. Howard described Dave as a "Reggae guy with hair like Whoopie Goldberg." Dave was not only personable, but quite knowledgeable. He explained the symbols adorning the interior of the building, and we were surprised to learn that although igloos formerly represented Eskimos (Inuits), Alaskan Inuits don't live in igloos; igloos are found only in the Arctic area of *Canada*. For Alaska, igloos now represent tourism.

Dave also pointed out a bronze statue of Elizabeth Peratrovich, a pioneer in Native rights. Incensed by signs in restaurant windows proclaiming, "No Natives, No Filipinos, No Dogs," Peratrovich, a Tlingit of the Raven Clan, vowed to end such blatant discrimination. Her impassioned speech in the Alaska state senate convinced legislators and the governor to pass the anti-discrimination bill in February of 1945. This legislation was enacted almost twenty years before the National Civil Rights Act of 1964. February 16 is now celebrated annually as Elizabeth Peratrovich Day.

After leaving the Capitol, we lunched at McDonald's, then re-re-boarded the trolley. This time we got off at the State Museum, where another Dave was our guide. He showed us an exhibit depicting the last battle of the Civil War, which happened to take place in Alaska—one of several skirmishes that occurred after Lee's surrender at Appomattox in April of 1865.

Captain James Waddell, under orders from the Confederate Naval Department, cruised the Pacific specifically targeting Union whaling fleets. On June 28, 1865, he captured twenty-five American whalers in the Bering Sea. Crews from the whalers were taken aboard the CSS Shenandoah before their vessels were burned. They were later put ashore or taken to port on another vessel. It wasn't until Capt. Waddell eventually arrived in Liverpool, England (seven months after Appomattox, and 23,000 miles from the Aleutians), that he acknowledged the end of the war and lowered his Confederate flag.

Tuesday we visited the Shrine of St. Therese, which Connie had told us was a good site for whale-watching. We watched some distant rocks for half an hour before realizing they weren't going to turn into whales.

Wednesday morning we stopped at the City Museum primarily to get out of the rain, but we found the museum to be a treasure.

One hands-on exhibit for children featured an old toybox with this question posted above it: "Was there fun before TV?"

The displays from old newspapers were especially fascinating in light of current events. One article on "Seward's folly" quoted a congressman who considered it "a crime to take money from coffers of widows and orphans to pay for this vast white elephant called Alaska." We read another article on the evils of cigarette smoking:

> "Parents should look closely after their children, as it is not an unusual thing to see a number of small boys ranging in age from eight to twelve years under some house or some waterfront foundations smoking cigarettes. The cigarette habit is a most abominable one and ruins the health of many young boys . . . ."
>
> *Juneau City Mining Record*, 1892

SKAGWAY, ALASKA—June 19-22, 1997

Friday afternoon we left Juneau aboard the Taku (the nicest ferry of our trip). This was the first time we'd sailed during so many daylight hours and the first clear day. We could see long ranges of white-capped mountains on both sides of the channel. We also saw half a whale (the tail-half), as it disappeared into the water.

We arrived at our campground, only fifteen blocks north of the ferry terminal, shortly before midnight. This was the welcome beginning of several days of warm *dry* weather, and we were glad for a chance to air out our RV.

It was 80° in the shade at 8:00 the next night. We kept waiting for the sun to go down so it would cool off. Here it was, only one day after the summer solstice, and we'd already forgotten that the famed midnight sun doesn't exactly set. We had about three hours of semi-darkness each night we were there, usually beginning about 1:00 a.m.

One morning we took a walking tour with a Park Ranger, Scott Tucker. Scott showed us the home of Skagway founder, Mr. Moore, who, among other things, worked for the Yukon post office, carrying mail at age 75 in minus-75° weather. Moore foresaw the gold rush ten years before it began, and also had the foresight to tell his son to save their house, which he realized would someday be famous.

Scott explained the requirements for joining the Arctic Brotherhood: (1) climb the Chilkoot Trail, or (2) be a gold-digger in one way or another (pun intended).

That afternoon we took a "Bushwhack tour" of the ghost town of Old Dyea, where the legendary Chilkoot Trail began. This steep and treacherous passage was made famous during the Klondike goldrush. We climbed only a short stretch of the trail—enough to gain our respect for the goldminers who roughed it nearly a century ago in frigid weather and deep snow.

ON THE ROAD—June 23-29, 1997

The only way to get from Skagway to central Alaska by land is to cut diagonally across the southwest corner of Canada, mostly through Yukon Territory. The very name conjures images of rugged wilderness. There aren't many routes from Whitehorse YT into Alaska, and we chose the southern highway that goes through Kluane Lake, enjoying bright displays of wild sweetpea and fireweed along the way.

When we crossed from Canada into Alaska, the US border inspector wanted to know if we were bringing in more than $10,000 in cash. We Front-Rangers must look quite wealthy.

Our first overnight stop was at Deadman's Lake, where we battled mosquitoes. It was a short drive the next day to Tok, which is sort of a crossroads leading to either Fairbanks or Anchorage. After getting fishing info from a game biologist who admitted he knew more about game than fish, Howard took a long swampy walk before reaching a remote lake four miles north of Tok. Once there, he saw Mama and Baby Moose approaching and cut his fishing excursion short.

FAIRBANKS, ALASKA
June 30 through July 6, 1997

We found a nice RV park in the town of North Pole, just outside Fairbanks. Right before we reached town, we slowed down to a crawl for a moose who was lumbering down the exact center of the highway. Guess he figured he got here first and wasn't about to hurry along for the likes of us. He finally moved aside and let us travel on.

Hope you don't think we came to Alaska to cool off! This is as far north as we'll be going, and probably the warmest we'll get. One article in the Fairbanks newspaper began, "Now serving—baked Alaska." The high on July 1 was 85°, higher than the high in Hilo, Hawaii; Lansing, Michigan; or New York City (all 83°). No sympathy from the folks in Albuquerque (97°) or Phoenix (104°).

We visited the highly touted Santa Claus House, which I found disappointing compared to the lovely Christmas shop in Pigeon Forge. We also drove to the LARS (Large Animal Research Station) hoping to see musk ox. We saw one (1).

The State Museum had some excellent exhibits, including a program on the Northern Lights and a haunting display about the relocation of Aleuts and Japanese-Americans during WWII.

One day while we were out, the wind blew down our small American flag (the one we'd bought at K-Mart for $1.50), and a little three-year-old boy discovered it. He marched around with it *constantly* the next couple of days. It was fun for us to see him getting so much pleasure from it, so we didn't even try to reclaim it.

We bought groceries and a new flag at Fred Meyers, then celebrated Independence Day by watching the Boston Pops special on TV. Howard barbecued steak and halibut; the asparagus cost more than both together.

We toured the Alyeska pipeline, or rather one small segment of it. Evelyn, our guide, was very friendly, and after the tour we enjoyed chatting with her about the pipeline and other aspects of living in Alaska. She explained that you won't find graffiti or vandalism around the pipeline, because children are taught to understand that this is the source of the generous annual reimbursement to every citizen of the state.

She also told us about her children's school and winter conditions: When the temperature reaches 30° BELOW zero, kids stay indoors for recess—above that, they play outside. When it reaches 55° below, parents have the option of sending their kids to school or not—the buses are still running. When it reaches 60° below, the buses stop running.

Summertime brings its own unique possibilities, she told us. The Matanuska Valley, northeast of Anchorage, is famous for growing giant vegetables, and farmers hold contests to see who can raise the largest. "Enormous" would be an understatement: Cabbages too large to fit through a hula hoop, tomatoes the size of pumpkins, broccoli over three feet tall—this is just a small sampling. Although the growing *season* is short (June through August), the summer *days* are long, and gardens flourish under twenty-four daily hours of sunshine.

Evelyn described her tiny elderly grandmother, who takes advantage of the midnight sun to cultivate her own garden. Neighboring moose also take advantage of this time to devour her garden. Grandma—obviously not intimidated by these monstrous beasts—gets so mad at them, she literally chases them away, waving her broom as she runs, her long gray braids flying behind her.

DENALI NATIONAL PARK—July 7-13, 1997

When the park service designated Denali a national park, they relied on what they'd learned from other national parks. In order to keep it a wilderness and a preserve, much of the park is closed to the public. Harmony between animals and people is maintained thanks in part to the control of traffic. There is one road into Denali, ending at Kantishna, ninety miles to the west, with limited private access. Tour and shuttle buses are the only vehicles allowed beyond a certain point.

Our park-service guide at the Visitor Center explained the rules of bear encounters: Make lots of noise and talk loudly. "It doesn't matter what you say. '*I want my mommy*' works," he said.

We took the bus tour through the park Wednesday, with the weather cooperating. Our tour guide and driver, Ruth, was friendly and well-informed.

Naturally, we saw a lot of wildlife. Especially interesting to me was a ptarmigan fanning its white tail feathers, as well as several hoary marmots (which looked like large Persian cats from a distance), and a male grizzly standing and stretching—"showing off."

At one point where we stopped, we were supposed to get a good view of Mt. Denali (formerly Mt. McKinley). The summit was obscured, but we did see the middle third. (Not too exciting.)

What *was* exciting was seeing a grizzly bear family so close to our bus we didn't need binoculars. The sow was blonde; one of the cubs was blond; the other, dark brown. The mother was busy eating wild grass and didn't seem to pay much attention to the cubs, who were busy cavorting and scuffling with each other.

After Ruth stopped the bus so people could take pictures, all three crossed the road in front of us. One cub stayed close to the bus and vocalized—more of a soft groan than a growl. Ruth said this was only the second time in the ten years she'd been conducting tours that she'd ever heard this. We saw the same bear family farther up the road. Ruth told us the bears in this area are smaller than average because there's no salmon—their diet is 90% vegetation.

That evening in our campground, Ranger Stacy gave a presentation on "The Effect of Light on Plants, Animals, and People." She suggested an interesting experiment: spending a day without clocks. This made us realize how accustomed we are to keeping track of time—even in our nomadic lifestyle.

The next afternoon we met with Ranger Larry for a hike to the training area for sled dogs. The dogs gave an exciting demonstration of their ability to run and work together. They're bred for friendliness as well as for pulling sleds, and interact well with people. Ranger Greg explained that some people think working sled dogs are a thing of the past, but these dogs have an ongoing job, bringing supplies to remote areas.

TALKEETNA, ALASKA—July 15-16, 1997

By following a paved spur road off the main highway between Fairbanks and Anchorage for fourteen miles, we reached Talkeetna. We especially liked this rugged town that reminded us of Silverton, Colorado, or maybe the mythical Cicely, Alaska, on *Northern Exposure*. Talkeetna is a starting point for people who've come to scale Mt. Denali. The Park Service gives extensive training and survival courses for climbers.

The next morning began with yelling and banging coming from the outhouse at our campground. Howard then rescued a little Native boy about six years old who'd gotten locked inside. Afterwards, without a word, the little boy jumped on his bike and rode off like a shot.

Howard fished, then we went into town again. At the schoolhouse, Ranger Maureen explained the diorama of Denali and the surrounding mountains. We then returned to the Ranger Station, which was new—had a homey lounge area with a big fireplace, comfy chairs. Along the ceiling were flags left by different groups from all over the world who'd tried climbing the mountain.

As we were leaving Talkeetna, we looked in the rear-view mirror, and—thanks to the clear weather—could discern a gray mountain range we hadn't been able to see yesterday. Hoping to get a glimpse of Mr. Denali, which is usually obscured by clouds, we stopped at the lookout point to look back at the mountains. The range resembled a gray cardboard silhouette and, to our untrained eyes, all the peaks appeared pretty much alike.

Then we noticed "an interesting cloud formation" well above the range. When the "cloud" didn't drift away even after we'd stared at it for a while, we realized we were actually seeing a startlingly clear view of Mt. Denali! We were truly awed. There were clouds about half-way down, which seemed to blend into the snow-capped summit *far* above the gray range. The top third looked suspended from the sky by invisible wires, disconnected from the lower part.

Also viewing were a couple from Missouri, and a young amateur photographer from Singapore who hadn't recognized Denali at first either, even though he'd been taking pictures of it for several years. We all felt we'd celebrated something very special together.

EKLUTNA AND EAGLE RIVER, ALASKA
Saturday, July 19, 1997

Today we visited St. Nicholas Russian Orthodox Church in the town of Eklutna. We were fascinated by the spirit houses in the small cemetery there—rows of wooden structures the size of caskets built horizontally over graves. But there was nothing gloomy about them. Families took great care to provide colorful and attractive houses, each one brightly decorated so that the spirit of the departed loved one would have a cheerful place to return to.

Next we visited St. John the Evangelist Antiochian Orthodox Church in Eagle River. It was surrounded by woods and green rolling hills, reminding us of Maggie Valley, North Carolina. No people were around when we approached the church, but an amiable golden retriever kept us company while we sat on a bench enjoying the peaceful view.

The sound of an ice-cream truck brought Fr. Marc Dunaway and his wife, Betsy, running outside from their home next door. They were very cordial and invited us to attend their service the next day. We explained about our home on wheels, plus not being able to "dress up." They waved away our concerns over clothes, and told us we could park our RV in their driveway.

From there we traveled ten unpaved miles down a washboard road to find Eklutna Lake Recreational Park, which we'd heard was popular with Alaskans. We were happy to find both lovely scenery and friendly campers. Our evening entertainment was spotting Dall sheep and hiking to a lake to view a glacier.

EAGLE RIVER AND ANCHORAGE, ALASKA
Sunday, July 20, 1997

We got up early, hitched up, and drove our Front Range to the Dunaways' driveway so we could attend morning liturgy. This was the first Eastern Orthodox service either of us had ever attended, and we found it very moving. The parishioners welcomed us and invited us to join them outside for lemonade afterwards.

From there it was a short drive to Anchorage. The first place we visited was Earthquake Park, where there were supposed to be interpretive displays about the devastating earthquake of 1964. All we found were people looking puzzled over the lack of displays. So we settled for enjoying the hike and nice weather instead.

Tonight we saw a slide presentation about The Great Earthquake—a magnitude 9.2 quake that lasted a terrifying five minutes on Good Friday of 1964 and virtually destroyed Anchorage and Valdez. The epicenter was in Prince William Sound, southwest of Valdez, and the quake was felt for several hundred miles. Some neighborhoods in Anchorage were completely swept into the Pacific.

The subsequent tsunami waves were felt as far away as Japan and California, and caused more fatalities (106 in Alaska and 16 in California and Oregon) than the earthquake itself (nine—all in Alaska). Most of the powerful tsunamis reached about 50 feet in height, but one near Valdez was recorded at 219 feet.

Both Anchorage and Valdez have since been rebuilt—once again illustrating the courage and resilience of Alaskan residents. We found the downtown area of Anchorage well-landscaped with an abundance of flowers, many spilling over from hanging baskets—cheerful and modern.

SOLDOTNA THROUGH VALDEZ, ALASKA
July 22 through August 4, 1997

In Soldotna, Howard caught several rainbow-hued Dolly Varden trout within five minutes of fishing on the Kenai. The Kenai is a beautiful milky aqua color and is very cold.

One afternoon we took a drive through the most gorgeous profuse fields of fireweed we encountered throughout our entire trip. The flowers of the fireweed are bright pink, and the plants we saw had grown to well over three feet high.

In Homer, we stayed at a park called Oceanview, but couldn't view too much of the ocean due to fog and low tide. We drove out to Homer Spit, which looks like (fill in rhyming word). Miles of RVs cluttered together every which way. When the weather cleared, we discovered mountains, and blue water, putting the town itself in an attractive setting.

Seward was a charming town. While there, we took a cruise on Resurrection Bay with nine or ten other passengers. We had the pleasure of seeing otters at play, as well as puffins and kittiwakes. At the beginning of our trip, the sky was bright blue, the sea turquoise; but when the fog came in, the colors became gently muted.

We also visited Exit Glacier, which is known to have easy access. However there was too much runoff for visitors to get as close as they had in the past. Still, we could walk close enough to get a good view. The color was quite impressive, with amazing royal-blue crevasses in the light-aqua glacier.

On our way out, we picked up three hitchhikers from Tempe, Arizona. Back home, picking up hitchhikers is unwise; but here, where it's easy for folks to get stranded, it seems natural.

As we traveled on, we began to see lots of "ex-fireweed" on the side of the road and realized that summer was coming to an end. While Sitka was my favorite Alaskan town, Valdez was Howard's. He had fun fishing there—caught ten nice-sized salmon, some as long as his arm. By our last day, his arm was tired.

LAKE TESLIN CAMPGROUND, YUKON TERRITORY
August 8, 1997

When we stopped in Teslin, we had no idea it would be such an interesting stay. Having nothing better to do, we visited the G.J. Johnston Museum—what a treat! Although George Johnston was a Tlingit with strong Native ties, he had very modern ideas.

An enterprising photographer, he took scores of photos in the 1940s depicting life in those times. Besides the photographs, the museum housed his 1928 Chevrolet. What made this car unique was that George had it sent 300 miles by steamship, and there weren't even any roads to drive it on. So George and his friends built a 3-mile stretch of road so they could enjoy "George's taxi"— quite a novelty in its day.

WATSON LAKE, YT—August 9, 1997

We visited the famed "Signpost Forest," with its overwhelming display of more than 30,000 signs that people from all over the world have placed there. The custom began when a homesick soldier, Carl Lindley, who was working on the Alaska Highway during World War II, erected a lone sign pointing to his hometown, Danville, Illinois. Other soldiers added their signs, little realizing the tradition they had started.

Today's colorful signs vary in shape and size, but most are about the size of license plates and are made of wood or metal. Visitors can have their own signs made at the site. We knew the Woodards and Stoltes had placed one from Zapata when they visited, and it took us most of the afternoon to find it. In the meantime, it was a pleasant surprise to find the sign Connie and Wayne Butaud had left. It was fun to feel we had touched base with our "ferry friends" again.

KINASKAN PROVINCIAL PARK, BRITISH COLUMBIA
August 10, 1997

It took us a *long* time to bump down the decrepit Stewart-Cassiar Highway to Kinaskan. Early in the day we stopped at Beaver Creek rest area, where we read one sign saying it was a *2-hour drive* to Iskut, and another that it was 244 km (*150 miles*) to Iskut. We figured we'd need to drive 75 mph to reach Iskut in two hours, which is ambitious for BC, and extremely optimistic for the Cassiar Highway. We were passed only once by someone who might achieve that dubious goal. *Five hours later*, we arrived in Iskut.

We traveled another seventy miles to Kinaskan, which is the most beautiful provincial park we've stayed in so far. It was too late in the afternoon to find sites by the sparkling blue lake, but the campsites on the opposite side were forested and equally nice. It was the first *dark* night we've had since leaving Albuquerque; we saw stars again for the first time in recent memory.

STEWART, BC, AND HYDER, ALASKA
August 11-12, 1997

We finally got pavement about twenty miles before reaching the turnoff to Stewart, where we found an RV park we liked. We saw a black bear cub on the side of road along the way, a sight that will never seem commonplace to me.

Stewart, British Columbia (population about 3,000), and Hyder, Alaska (population 85), are unlikely twin cities. The pavement ends at the Canadian side of the border. There are no customs officials when you enter the unpaved roads of Hyder, a quaint community that bills itself as "the friendliest little ghost town in Alaska." Because it's so small, it doesn't deal in American money. But it does stay in the Alaskan time zone. A little confusing, but not enough to matter.

We visited St. Paul's church—"the Smallest Orthodox Cathedral in the World." Then we shopped at Mom's This and That Shop—our last opportunity to buy Alaskan souvenirs.

We did have to go through Canadian customs as we re-entered Stewart on our return from Hyder. Our RV hosts had warned us to "look out for the redhead," when we crossed. Apparently he was the only grouch; fortunately, he wasn't on duty and our crossing went smoothly.

ROBSON MEADOWS PROVINCIAL PARK, BC
August 16, 1997

If yesterday was an uneventful day, today was *very* eventful! The towns along the Yellowhead Highway in central British Columbia are few and far between. There were ninety miles between our last stop (Prince George) and McBride. About thirty miles before we reached McBride, we saw a camper stranded on the side of the road. It turned out to be a family from Germany—a husband and wife and their two teenage sons. They told us, "Our petrol is all."

So we drove Birgid into town while her husband and sons stayed behind with their camper. She was a delightful person, and we quickly felt like old friends. She spoke English fairly well, and was pleased that Howard knew a few phrases in German. At one point she asked if our truck was new, and Howard replied, "Pretty new."

"Ya," she said, nodding solemnly. "It's pretty. And it's new." I couldn't help laughing out loud, but didn't know how to explain. I wondered if she thought we felt compelled to brag to everyone about our pretty truck.

When we reached McBride, we were reluctant to leave Birgid until the gas station attendant assured us it would be easy to find a ride back to her family.

As we approached Mt. Robson, the highest point in the Canadian Rockies, we considered ourselves lucky to get a good view of this peak, which—like Mt. Denali—isn't always visible.

We camped at Robson Meadows Provincial Park. That evening we attended a ranger program, which was fun even though the rain drove everyone—dogs and all—to the shelter of the amphitheater, where we shared rather close quarters.

We saw a clever skit about Ranger Janet and "Wayward Jeannie," designed to teach children the importance of safety in hiking. The children in the crowd were asked what might happen as a result of poor planning. One kid's repeated drastic prediction (with minor variations): "An animal might push a rock on Wayward Jeannie and squash her."

HOMEWARD BOUND
August 17 through September 5, 1997

We enjoyed our brief stays at Jasper, Lake Louise, and Banff National Parks. The most fascinating aspect of our visits was seeing elk wander in and out of the campground at Jasper as casually as domestic animals. At Banff, we took a hike to see the Hoodoos, immense "spooky" rock formations that are said to resemble primitive gods.

On Thursday, August 21, we crossed the border (yea!) without incident (yea again!)—except we couldn't bring in oranges, so we ate the remaining one on the Canadian side.

The following Saturday, we stayed at a campground in Great Falls, Montana. We were surprised to discover another Front Range parked there! First time we had ever seen another besides ours. The "Bounder" people and other motorhome owners have formed clubs that host big rallies from time to time. We thought maybe we should have a rally with the other Front Ranger, but we couldn't find anyone at home.

We arrived in Dillon to find the Beaverhead County Fair in progress. We had fun watching a cat show presented by the 4-H girls. These weren't highfalutin purebred cats, but regular house cats. Still, we were impressed at the way the girls demonstrated what they'd learned about caring for their pets.

ALBUQUERQUE AND PHOENIX
September through mid-November, 1997

September and October in Albuquerque mean the State Fair and the Balloon Fiesta. Our favorite time of year to be anywhere, but especially here.

Howard and I got a big kick out of watching—and I do mean watching—our granddaughter Elliana, who was a year old in July. As Howard says, she just toddles around the house, smiling and mumbling to herself. Her vocabulary is rather limited: She calls all the Disney characters "Pooh," including Bambi.

We left Albuquerque mid-October with people/things still unseen/undone, and headed for Phoenix. Although I've never lived there, *wherever* Mom and Pop lived always had the feel of "home."

When we lived in Midland, Pop explained the game of baseball to me, and we spent many a summer evening at the ball park. He taught me how to ride a bicycle when I was nine, and how to drive a car when I was thirteen (which would have been a hair-raising experience, I'm sure, if he'd had more hair). He taught my cousin Bee and me to play poker and Michigan rummy.

I'm grateful to him for all the things he led me to appreciate (some that I didn't appreciate at the time). His love of life, which included his convictions, his patriotism, his curiosity, his sense of humor, his sense of history: What a wonderful gift to all of us!

My relationship with Mom was stormy at times, but in these later years those times fade away. Maybe one of her greatest gifts is that she always had *time* for us. Time, when we were small, to sing lullabies and read stories. Time, as we grew older, just to spend time.

And though Pop is gone now, and Mom's living arrangements have changed, the nostalgia remains. Now Linda's family helps keep the feeling of home alive.

I began reading James Michener's *Alaska* while we were in Albuquerque. I got as far as Page 4 before it was due back at the library. So I checked it out again in Phoenix. This time I got to Page 8 before it was due. When I left them, the terranes were still clashing around. I hope to get back to them "one of these days." Something tells me I'd better get my own copy.

ZAPATA, TEXAS
November 26 through December 31, 1997

Now that our Alaskan journey had ended, we were ready to move back into our Alpenlite, which suddenly seemed enormous compared to our little Front Range. Still, we had happy memories of the roads we'd traveled in it and weren't quite ready to part with it, thinking it might be useful for weekend trips. So we decided to store it at our RV park in Zapata for the time being.

As you can imagine, after being gone from our Alpenlite for eight months, we had some rearranging (and remembering) to do. Luckily, except for a thin layer of dust, it was pretty clean, especially considering we'd left a couple of vents and windows cracked for circulation. The biggest surprise: The cactus wrens had decided the ideal place to build a nest was between the window and the screen in the bathroom.

I was also surprised at how disoriented I felt at first. Couldn't remember where I used to keep things (or why). But eventually it all came back. And once it was livable again and our Christmas decorations in place, everything began to look quite festive, and we found ourselves looking up too.

1998

At the beginning of this year, we took a departure from our RV lifestyle by taking a ten-day tour of the Holy Land. We carpooled with other members of the tour group from Zapata to San Antonio, then flew from there to Israel via Chicago.

The whole journey was an amazing experience, but one of the highlights for Howard was actually standing with his friend Jerry at the Wailing Wall in Jerusalem, where he offered prayers for his parents as well as for my dad. It's hard to describe the emotional impact of simply being in such a revered place.

For me, one of the most moving experiences occurred in a cold dark cave in Bethlehem. When we entered the cave said to be the site of Jesus's birth, we huddled close together and listened as the familiar words from *Luke*'s Gospel came alive. Then, into the stillness, one of the girls from our group began singing *O Holy Night*. As her pure sweet voice filled the air, there wasn't a dry eye among us. And the tears continued as we all sang *Away in a Manger*, *O Little Town of Bethlehem*, and *Silent Night*, as if we were hearing the words for the first time.

Often as we walked through various streets, the sound of the muezzin calling Muslims to prayer would boom out over a loudspeaker. Many Muslims would gather in the square; but what impressed me most was seeing shopkeepers standing outside their shops, quietly fingering their prayer beads. Since it was hard to hear anything else, it seemed to me *everyone*—Muslim or otherwise—might as well stop to pray.

Our guide Hanna taught us to say "Good morning" in Hebrew: "Boker Tov." We had a hard time with this the first few days—our pronunciation sounded awkward and unnatural. I think we were all saying something like "Bokel Tov," and she warned the group that "bokel" means "rocking chair."

By the end of our trip, it came a little more easily, and people smiled and said, "Boker Tov" in return. I'm still not sure if they were smiling because they were pleased I was greeting them in Hebrew or because I was wishing them "good rocking chair."

*   *   *

Back in Zapata, I began volunteering at the Boys and Girls' Club, which was a blast. Will I ever forget Ana's enthusiasm for reading, and the way she fussed at Curious George when she read that he'd been naughty again. In fact, I was quite impressed with how well all the children could read—even the first graders. Somebody must be doing something right.

My favorable impression of the Zapata school system was reinforced when I visited the school exhibits at the Zapata County Fair, where a wide variety of talents and projects was displayed. One of the things that amused me: A class of fifth-graders had created biographies that listed their individual interests and goals. The goal of most of the girls was to visit Paris; that of the boys, to meet Michael Jordan.

Most retirees who live in Zapata during the winter head "north" before the triple-digit summer temps begin. This exodus usually occurs between March and May. We usually leave around the first of April, but this year our daughter Linda came to San Antonio the 20th of March for a week-long seminar, so we decided to leave earlier and meet her and our granddaughter Adrienne there. Adrienne stayed with us while Linda was seminaring, and we had perfect weather for doing the tourist stuff—visiting the Alamo, the zoo, the River Walk, the Mercado.

On top of all this, my cousin Rob treated us to second-row seats at a Spurs-Suns basketball game. Seeing the Spurs play—and win—was exciting in itself. But the size of the Alamodome with all its pizzazz was pretty mind-boggling—at least for us country mice.

From San Antonio we came "north" to Arizona for the month of April, then spent May in Albuquerque. We had fun baby-sitting Elliana one day. She is nearly two years old now, and everything is "mine" at that age. Before leaving the house, Mike told us he'd explained to her, "My stereo is *mine*, but she might try to convince you it's hers."

We spent Independence Day in Chama, which is fairly quiet except for the train as it makes its trip to Antonito and back. Still, it's a sound I like. I thought of Pop as we watched the Boston Pops 4th of July celebration on TV. How he enjoyed the Sousa marches.

Mid-July brought us to Gunnison again. This town is one of our favorites—very similar to Dillon in many ways. We enjoy taking walks through neighborhoods with picturesque Victorian-type homes, lots of flowers—red-orange California poppies and tall indigo delphiniums—and even taller evergreens.

One day while taking a walk, we saw two little girls about five years old playing outside their house. When they saw us coming, they started shrieking, "STRANGERS!!!! STRANGERS!!!!" and ran inside.

It was kind of funny, since we'd never thought of ourselves in that category. But we also felt sad that the world has become such a scary place for little people.

Blue Mesa RV Park is right across the street from Blue Mesa Reservoir. The lake is surrounded by mesas, which are somewhat barren and plain with very little vegetation. The patterns in the mesas make me think of "paint-by-the-number" pictures, with rather distinct markings in numerous shades of brown and gray. It's a unique beauty that has grown on me.

In the evening, when the sky is often dark with thunderclouds, the mesas take on a striking bluish-gray hue, and the lake becomes an even deeper blue. The cloud-streaked sky becomes multicolored, the sunsets spectacular.

*　　*　　*

People have sometimes asked us how we could stand to move away from our children. In truth, most of them flew the nest before we did and are scattered from Florida to Michigan to California to Hawaii. So there's no one place we could settle that would encompass everyone. Still, over the last few months, we have given more thought to slowing down and "putting down roots" again. Albuquerque seemed the logical place to relocate, not only because the majority of our kids and grandkids live there, but also because it's fairly close to our Phoenix family, and relatively central to everyone else.

In October, we made the decision to become "half-timers" instead of "full-timers" and bought a small but nice mobile home in Albuquerque. Now we have a home base, but we can still take off to travel from time to time. In fact, we plan to go back to Zapata shortly after the holidays. So our adventures aren't really coming to an end—they're simply taking another turn.

With the holidays in mind, our wish for you—for all of us—is that we continue to celebrate everything worthy of celebration, each day and always.

NEW MEXICO FAIR FLAVORS

Cotton-candied kids
    with flower-painted faces
        and Dr. Seuss hats

Splashy quilts
    and Tom Bollack pumpkins
        and Hatch green chili
          and lemonade

Macho guys armed with
    fuzzy pink bears
        they've won for their sweethearts
          in games of chance

Curvy girls
    wearing short swingy skirts
        and tall springy hair
          and hiking boots
            with bunchy socks

Acomita preschoolers
    munching on fair fare
        while sporting feathered headbands
          by Mutual of Omaha

Buffalo dancers
  and Buffalo soldiers
    and Mariachis
      and Methodist pies

Sleeping babies
  curled over strollers
    or draped across shoulders
      of

Sturdy daddies
  holding small sticky fingers
    of wide-eyed toddlers
      while

Sun-warmed mommies
  embrace the excitement
    and breathe thanks to God
      for

Cotton-candied kids . . . .

MAPS & PHOTOS

Although the maps on the following pages aren't drawn to any kind of scale, I hope they'll be helpful as guides to our various destinations.

East Canyon Resort, Henefer, Utah

"Freddy the Freeloader," Zapata, Texas

Float entered in Zapata County parade

Los Ebanos Ferry, Texas/Mexico border

Howard and "The Big Tree" on Goose Island, Texas

Pigeon Forge, Tennessee

Howard and Valerie fishing in Zapata

Valerie's catch

Julius building his fish at Bass Lake RV Park

Memories of Zapata County Boys & Girls' Club

Margaret in Luckenbach, Texas

Smallest International Bridge in North America
(between US & Canada in the 1000 Islands)

Alaska Bound in the Front Range

Sled Dog Demo at Denali National Park